It Was 40 Years Ago Today

Thomas Dresser

PublishAmerica
Baltimore

© 2009 by Thomas Dresser.
All rights reserved. No part of this book may be reproduced, stored in a retrieval system or transmitted in any form or by any means without the prior written permission of the publishers, except by a reviewer who may quote brief passages in a review to be printed in a newspaper, magazine or journal.

First printing

ISBN: 1-60610-420-9
PUBLISHED BY PUBLISHAMERICA, LLLP
www.publishamerica.com
Baltimore

Printed in the United States of America

Foreword

Sarah climbed up the steps of my school bus, all her middle-school hopes and dreams stuffed in a tote bag casually slung over her shoulder. The black bag bore the iconic words: "The Beatles." A few stops later, Caitlyn clambered aboard, wearing a faded Beatles T-shirt. Austin, a rising sophomore was attired in a John Lennon T-shirt: "Give Peace a Chance." These kids' parents were probably not born when The Beatles sang together. Would I have worn something from my father's generation?

Martha's Vineyard's West Tisbury eighth grade class, all twenty-two of them, stood together at their graduation at the Agricultural Hall. They sang the poignant, "Hello Goodbye," which captured their moment, looking at their past, as they stepped forward.

Joyce and I were in Bed & Bath in Los Angeles, moseying along the aisles. "I Saw Her Standing There" came over the speakers. We glanced at each other, then started to dance.

When Howard Schultz returned to revitalize Starbucks, in the winter of 2008, he encouraged management to reinvent the greatness of the coffee giant. He began a retreat, listening to The Beatles, a prime ingredient in his motivational recipe.

The Ohio State Glee Club sang *Eleanor Rigby*, sandwiched between college cheers and classical sonatas. Vineyard Sound, an a cappella group, opened their season with the haunting "Here, There and Everywhere."

Paul McCartney was awarded an honorary degree as a Doctor of Music at the 2008 Yale graduation ceremony.

Steve Emerson, nationally respected expert on current mores, considered the Internet the most significant change in communication since…The Beatles held the world in their hands.

In 2008 the songs of The Beatles are as alive as ever. This book is a tribute to the longevity of their tunes and the influence of their music. Besides personal memories, we reference Songfacts and Wikipedia for background data on The Beatles' vast repertoire, and add impressions with little help from our friends.

Thomas Dresser
Martha's Vineyard
Spring, 2009

Dedication

This book is dedicated to my loving wife of ten years, Joyce, whose patience and support carried me through this project. I am eternally grateful for her encouragement.

Table of Contents

Preface 11
Introduction 14
Chapter One: Please Please Me—March 22, 1963 16
Chapter Two: With the Beatles—November 22, 1963 23
Chapter Three: Hard Day's Night—July 10, 1964 28
Chapter Four: Beatles for Sale—December 4, 1964 36
Chapter Five: Help!—August 6, 1965 46
Chapter Six: Rubber Soul—December 3, 1965 52
Chapter Seven: Revolver—August 5, 1966 65
Chapter Eight: Sgt. Pepper's Lonely Hearts Club Band—June 1, 1967 ... 90
Chapter Nine: The White Album—November 22, 1968 134
Chapter Ten: Let It Be (recorded January 1969)—Released May 8, 1970 155
Chapter Eleven: Abbey Road—September 26, 1969 175
Epilogue: It Was 40 Years Ago Today 187

*With your stereo blasting,
sit down and enjoy a trip down memory lane.*

Preface

In June 1964 I heard from DJ Murry the K on WINS radio in NYC, that on August 28, 1964, at Forest Hills Tennis Stadium in Queens, that the Beatles would be performing. I was sixteen years old, and had been among the many infected by Beatlemania. From "I Want to Hold Your Hand" on, I was hooked by their exuberance. Each new song hit the radio like a bomb. Stations took to playing new singles of theirs twice in a row because the audience was ravenous.

It was exciting to hear of the concert, because my Aunt Lomas lived about 10 miles from us in Forest Hills, not far from the stadium. I called and asked her to get me 2 tickets. She said, sure. My Aunt thought, as did I, that she would simply walk over there and buy them. But she went and joined a long line, and slowly (I think it took 2 hours) got to the ticket booth and purchased the tickets. I was truly grateful she'd stuck it out.

At the stadium we were seated in a crowd of 14,000. Other acts, Jackie De Shannon, the Righteous Brothers, the Cookies, and others, performed 2 or 3 songs each (just their hits) before the Beatles' helicopter arrived.

The Beatles ran to their positions and began playing, but you could hardly hear them. What you could hear was an extended roar that, for 30 minutes (that was the length of their set) was the primal sound of maybe 10,000 young people (I know I wasn't screaming but my girlfriend was), overcome with ecstatic energy from being in proximity to the Fab Four.

It was deafening and draining, but I watched as John, Paul, George, and Ringo mimed (so it seemed) their set while girls were writhing, screaming, and crying continuously. With a modern sound system they most likely would've been heard, but this was in the earliest era of outdoor rock concerts, and sound was fairly primitive.

On that day probably only those in the first 10 rows heard much of their music and singing. At the time, the way I described it was— it was like being near a jet airplane taking off— for 30 minutes. It was thrilling to be in the midst of so much human energy generated by 4 young men in their early 20s. I knew at that time, I was at the center of the universe.

—Richard Skidmore
Aquinnah, Massachusetts
Spring, 2008

I've loved The Beatles and their music since they first stood American popular culture on its ear, early in 1964. Along with countless others, I watched them on the Ed Sullivan Show that Sunday night in February. The whole family watched. Do whole families ever watch the same show together anymore? Do variety shows, for that matter, exist any more?

It has been said that the music one hears as an adolescent is the music that leaves the most lasting impression, and that that music remains ever green in memory. If it's so, I'm grateful that The Beatles (and their contemporaries) were the soundtrack of my adolescent years. I was twelve when they appeared on the Sullivan Show, and eighteen when they broke up in 1970. What a ride we all had!

I heard Melanie's version of "Any Time at All" for the first time today. That song has always been one of my favorites among the less famous Beatles tracks. I never tire of hearing that piano bridge. Melanie's version was fine, but (as is the case with so many cover versions) it reminded me how great the original was. Another Beatles cover I heard for the first time this week was "Yesterday," as done by Jerry Murad's Harmonicats. I confess I wasn't sure what to think; before I had time to collect my thoughts, Jerry and the Cats had moved on to "A Taste of Honey." Whew!

I reckon that once The Beatles have got hold of you, they never let go. That's fine with me.

—Alan Degutis
Holden, Massachusetts
Spring 2008

Introduction

It is early 1964. I am seventeen. It's Sunday evening, and I'm babysitting for a family friend.

We did not have a television when I was growing up. My parents thought it was a bad influence. So here I am, at a neighbor's house, watching TV.

The Ed Sullivan show is on. The featured act is the new British singing group, The Beatles. Ed Sullivan tries to keep the crowd calm, to no avail. Excitement mounts. Can they meet my expectations?

"And here they are, ladies and gentlemen, THE BEATLES!"

Pandemonium breaks out. The sound of their songs is lost in the hysteria of the audience. I stand mesmerized by the television set, unbelieving, taking it all in, hoping this moment of incredible infatuation will last a lifetime.

And it has.

So began the American phase of The Beatles' career. Promoted by the mass media, talented in their own way, The Beatles never let fame cramp their style. They handled their position as spokesmen of the youth movement masterfully, blending talent, humor, and honesty to get their message across.

The Beatles wrote songs that sold to a most receptive audience, the generation born between 1945 and 1965, with adherents of all ages. The Beatles spoke to, as well as for, young people, the disillusioned yet idealistic youth not content with middle-class affluence, the bomb, the conflict of war, racial strife, hunger, and poverty. As spokesmen for the post-World War II baby-boomers, The Beatles engaged their audience with simple love songs, which evolved into social statements.

This is my take on their story, with a little help from my friends.

* * *

Joyce Dresser (retired teacher, spouse of author): *"I have always been an Elvis fan from the minute I saw him on Ed Sullivan. But then, in 1964 I saw the Beatles on Ed Sullivan and knew the American music scene was in for exciting times. They were all just too cute and innocent at that time. They all looked a little awe-struck by the magnitude of the excitement they generated in the US. Their early music was pure and innocent and gave us a look into their lives across the 'pond.' Hearing those songs now takes me back to a time when life was simpler in the US.*

"I was thrilled to visit The Beatles Museum in Liverpool and dance in a replica of the Cavern, their first venue. "I Want to Hold Your Hand" blared from the speakers, and all the chaperones of this 8th-grade trip began dancing. The kids watched in amazement as their stodgy teachers let loose. It was too much fun!

"The Beatles were cute, fun, and created some wonderful music. I enjoyed them immensely. However, Elvis is still the king. The Beatles are the princes."

Chapter One: *Please Please Me*—March 22, 1963

US release: Introducing The Beatles—January 10, 1964;
Early Beatles—March 22, 1965

It is the autumn of 1963. Outside it is dark, as if a storm is brewing, and the bright fluorescent lights emit an unnatural glow on the group of high school juniors clustered in our home room. We gather before the bell to compare notes on the British invasion. Debbie Hinckley, dishwater blond hair to her shoulders, confidently predicts great things for the Dave Clarke Five. I say, without hesitation, "I'm with The Beatles. They're going all the way."

John, Paul, George, and Ringo were born and raised in Liverpool on the west coast of England, a rough seaport city with a depressed economy and a cathedral bombed by German air raids in the Battle of Britain in World War II.

In 1956 16-year-old John Lennon formed a skittles group called the Quarrymen. Paul McCartney heard about the group and sought to join. A faded photograph shows the first time John and Paul sang together as gangly teenagers. Paul, in turn, brought along another school chum, George Harrison, and the group evolved into the Silver Beatles. Beatles was a play on the name of another group, the Crickets.

IT WAS 40 YEARS AGO TODAY

The Beatles played Liverpool nightclubs, making a name for themselves at the Cavern. They toured in the north of England, but their first break came with a trip to Hamburg, Germany, in 1960 to play in a beer hall. They didn't last long, however, as George Harrison's work permit was revoked because he was underage. He was just seventeen.

They returned to Hamburg the next year and played on stage up to eight hours at a time, in front of a relentless audience. They struggled to master their musical skills and wondered if there was a future for them in music.

The Beatles recorded a song in Hamburg, "My Bonnie," which caught the ear of an English music-store businessman, one Brian Epstein. He tracked down The Beatles when they returned to Liverpool and soon became their manager, promising to bring them success. He polished their act, dressed them in matching outfits, and coordinated their performance, which continued at the Cavern.

The Beatles needed a recording contract. Epstein secured a studio recording session with Decca Records on New Year's Day, 1962. Unfortunately (for Decca) The Beatles were deemed unremarkable, hence unmarketable. Disheartened, but not discouraged, John Lennon, Paul McCartney, George Harrison, Stu Sutcliffe, and Pete Best were confident they would succeed. As Lennon put it, he would lead the group to the "toppermost of the uppermost."

Even as opportunities arose, tragedy struck. Bass player Stu Sutcliffe suffered a brain aneurism and died in Hamburg. The tragedy had a sobering effect on the group, but did not dissuade them from their struggle for recognition.

A wire from Brian Epstein signaled a glimmer of hope. He had arranged another audition, this time with EMI and Parlophone Records. Epstein convinced EMI producer George Martin that The Beatles had the potential to play songs that would sell. A recording session was scheduled for June 6, 1962, in the Abbey Road studio in London.

George Martin liked what he heard, but made a significant suggestion. He wanted to replace The Beatles' drummer. Martin felt Pete Best lacked the personality, drive, and professionalism exhibited by John, Paul, and George. Brian Epstein agreed, and Best was replaced by Ringo Starr, a drummer of some renown, who knew The Beatles when he, too, had played in Hamburg, as a member of Rory Storm and the Hurricanes.

The Beatles were on the verge of rising from mediocrity to meteoric success.

When they had first met, Martin asked the young musicians to speak up if there was anything they didn't like. Without hesitation, George Harrison said he didn't care for Martin's necktie. Humor and bravado characterized The Beatles' ride to the pinnacle of the pop music world.

The first Beatle record, "Love Me Do," was released in September, 1962. The song has a catchy beat and a simple melody, featuring John on harmonica and backed by Ringo on tambourine. The record sold well, not only locally in Liverpool, but also across Britain.

To capitalize on the success of "Love Me Do," George Martin wanted The Beatles to record an old Cliff Richard tune, "How Do You Do It." The Beatles refused. Self-assurance was a key element in their career path. They preferred to record John's "Please Please Me," written in a style popularized by Roy Orbison. There was a determined method to The Beatles' dash to the top.

Brian Epstein handed the cast-off "How Do You Do It" to another group he managed, and Gerry and the Pacemakers took it to number one.

With "Please Please Me," George Martin realized The Beatles had an innate ear for what the market would bear. Their first album,

Please Please Me, released in March 1963, contained a variety of tunes. Eight of the fourteen songs on their first album were written by John Lennon and Paul McCartney. Featured singles were "Please Please Me" and "Love Me Do." The album stayed at the top of the charts for a remarkable thirty weeks in Great Britain.

Sales of "From Me to You" and "Thank You Girl" proved The Beatles had the skill, professionalism, and perseverance to maintain their place in the pop-music charts.

While touring England that summer of 1963 with Gerry and the Pacemakers and Roy Orbison, The Beatles reveled in fan adulation, showing they could hold their own with the best in the business. Cheering throngs greeted them at concerts, and fans relentlessly tossed jelly babies on stage. (George once casually mentioned that The Beatles had an affinity for this candy, which is softer than American jellybeans.) The Beatles had to employ a road manager, Mal Evans, from the Cavern, and an assistant, Neil Aspinall, to coordinate professional needs that came with their growing popularity.

Sitting on twin beds in a Newcastle hotel, John and Paul collaborated on a song that, more than any other, pushed them to the top of the music charts. "She Loves You" has a simple, repetitive lyric, told in the third person, with a catchy tune. It was recorded in July 1963, and maintained its position at the top of the British charts for nearly two months. "She Loves You" proved to be the best-selling Beatles single of all time. (Only McCartney's solo, "Mull of Kintyre," outsold it, decades later.)

That summer George Harrison was laid up for a few days in a Bournemouth hotel. He didn't want any visitors, and used this tranquil time to compose his first song, aptly titled, "Don't Bother Me." George sang in the style of Bill Haley, with a hauntingly honest, abrupt, yet moving manner. Song writing was becoming a Beatles trademark.

In October 1963 The Beatles performed at the London Palladium. The show was televised, with an audience estimated at some fifteen million. The next month they performed at the Royal Variety Show, with Queen Elizabeth in attendance. It was at that show John famously urged people in the cheaper seats to clap their hands and the rest of the audience to rattle their jewelry.

Beatlemania was born in Britain in the autumn of 1963.

Britain's *Musical Express* voted The Beatles the most popular music group of the year. Fleet Street hailed John Lennon and Paul McCartney as top composers of the year. The Beatles had introduced the Mersey beat, the sound of Liverpool, across Britain.

To reward their loyal legion of fans, The Beatles recorded a Christmas record, full of humor, personality, and charm. They sang a couple of Christmas tunes and revealed that what they enjoyed most was to retreat to the recording studio and work out the words and music to a new song. Their humor came through unabashedly and gave fan club members an intimate peek into their increasingly exciting lives.

To more fully grasp the strength of the group, a brief review of their individual personalities is in order.

John Winston Lennon, born October 9, 1940, gave The Beatles their initial impetus to succeed. He was their leader, both in mind and music. A sophisticated idealist, he saw life as it should be. Lennon was withdrawn, honest, well read, thoughtful, and unafraid to speak his mind, though he was often derided for doing so. He was the driving force behind The Beatles in the early years, most intent on achieving success.

James Paul McCartney was born on June 18, 1942. McCartney proved the most able agent for the group. He translated the criticism of Harrison and idealism of Lennon into a pragmatic statement. McCartney was outgoing, talkative, and enjoyed the fans. He acted as the spokesman, the interpreter to the outside world. A winsome bachelor through most of his Beatle years, McCartney's amused eyebrows, longing eyes, and cute smile were every teenage girl's dream.

Born February 25, 1943, George Harrison stood in the background, with little to say. Harrison developed into a premier musician, experimenting with new instruments and styles. He was the critic, the dissenter, whose songs could attack subtly. With his concern for young people, Harrison was keenly aware of the impact The Beatles had on the youth movement.

Ringo Starr, born Richard Starkey on July 7, 1940, was the sad-sack jokester of the group, the most down to earth. Compared to the other three, his life as a Beatle was less hectic. While generally quiet, as he kept the beat during recording sessions, Starr was attuned to what the others sought, and often had an apt comment to improve a recording.

Ringo enlivened the group, bringing humor and humanity to the foursome, even as he stood out. While John, Paul, and George took the stage, each standing 5'11", Ringo was conspicuous behind his drum set, with his rings, big nose, and stood only 5'4". Ringo proved the catalyst to The Beatles' success.

Personalities of The Beatles emerged: John the intellectual, Paul the cute guy, George the silent one, and Ringo the funny man. Four talented, humorous, enthusiastic, and attractive musicians made up The Beatles. The group itself proved much more than the individuals. The Beatles became bigger than John, Paul, George, and Ringo as they wrote and recorded songs adored, admired, and appreciated by young people around the world.

And all that happened more than forty years ago.

* * *

Cynthia Riggs (author): *"The first time I heard The Beatles was when I was on a research vessel in Antarctica, and a research assistant played The*

Beatles over and over on his little turntable. I got to know them very well." She adds that it's *"fun to see Cruise 17 of the Eltanin immortalized because of the Beatle connection."*

Dr. William Talley (psychologist): *"Their music will last forever."*

Marcella Andrews (college student): *"The Beatles' music is timeless. The lyrics, most of them, are simple enough that there are so many ways to think about them. Every age can understand and relate to the songs. You can find a song for every emotion, every feeling, and every good and bad day. When a Beatles song comes on, it makes everything better."*

Chapter Two: *With the Beatles—* November 22, 1963

US release—Meet the Beatles—January 20, 1964
and The Beatles Second Album—April 10, 1964

It is early Friday afternoon, a gray November day. I am in my high-school geometry class, my desk the third one back in the second row. The principal's voice comes over the intercom. Mrs. Rowell sets her chalk down on the blackboard tray, and faces the class. Expectantly, we look up at the big black box on the wall and listen.

"President Kennedy has been shot in Dallas, Texas."

The room grows still, absolutely still.

Then, typical high school juniors, we have to compare notes. Steve Drawbridge turns in his seat ahead of me, "Why would anyone want to kill JFK?"

I say, "I'm sure they'll catch whoever did it. Right away."

It is November 22, 1963.

We will always remember where we were on that fateful afternoon.

For their second album, *With the Beatles*, The Beatles composed eight original songs, of which one was by George Harrison. Six covers of other songs were recorded, primarily Motown and rhythm and blues. This album pushed *Please Please Me* off the top of the charts and lasted an additional twenty-one weeks, giving The Beatles top billing for nearly a year in Great Britain.

Lennon and McCartney wrote virtually all of the hundred-plus songs recorded by The Beatles over their six-year career in the limelight. Eminently talented musicians, the two of them worked closely in the first years of their partnership. One got an inspiration, and the other completed the thought.

Many of their compositions were admittedly imitations of the styles of other popular singers and songs. If imitation is the highest form of flattery, then it was the fine art of flattery that Lennon and McCartney practiced. They had the unique ability to recreate the beat and style of another composer, akin to an artist painting in the style of a master. Except The Beatles quickly proved themselves the masters.

In the style of Motown, John Lennon wrote "Please Mr. Postman," with the catchy line, "deliver de letter, de sooner, de better." "Hold Me Tight" was a take off on a Smokey Robinson song. "Money" was written to capitalize on the success of "Twist and Shout," by Phil Medley and Bert Russell. The Beatles deprecated their own success when they sang "Money," while aping a song popularized by the Isley Brothers.

John was recognized for his choice of chords in the song "Not a Second Time." His work was compared to classical composers Mahler and Schubert. In an interview with *Playboy* years later, John said, "I am like a chameleon, influenced by whatever is going on. If Elvis can do it, I can do it. If the Everly Brothers can do it, me and Paul can."

Paul McCartney was equally capable as a composer. In "All My Loving," he proved his skill with words. He said good-bye to his lover, told her to close her eyes, when he kissed her, and promised he'd write her every day, expressing his love. The simplicity of this love song captured the hearts of his teenage audience.

In the early days, Ringo achieved popularity singing "Boys" in concert, but needed another tune. John composed "I Want to Be Your Man" for Ringo, but instead it was handed to another up-and-coming British pop group. It became the first hit for the Rolling Stones. The Beatles proved their competence as they tossed off a song for the competition. The rivalry between the Stones and The Beatles was legendary. Billy J. Kramer found success with Beatle compositions "I Call Your Name" and "Do You Want to Know a Secret." Peter and Gordon recorded "A World Without Love."

The Beatles built upon their past, singing songs of Fats Domino, Buddy Holly, Carl Perkins, and Little Richard. They incorporated elements of black music in their songs. In *Soul on Ice*, (McGraw-Hill, NY, 1968, p. 202) Eldridge Cleaver (1935-1998), the eloquent Black Panther, wrote of the impact of black musicians on the work of The Beatles: "But The Beatles were on the scene, injecting Negritude by the ton into the whites, in this post-Elvis Presley beatnik era of ferment."

Cleaver felt The Beatles took the rhythm of black music and repackaged it for their white audience. While maintaining the image of the mind through their words, The Beatles brought emotion and excitement to their tunes.

The Beatles appealed on a visceral level with their long hair. They represented a slight superiority in age over their audience. Most significantly, The Beatles stood out from other Liverpool Mersey groups because they composed as well as performed their own songs.

The Beatles wrote and sang songs that plucked the hearts and intrigued the minds of a generation born in the shadows of World War II. Why did this baby-boom generation adore four lower-middle-class lads from Liverpool? The phenomenon of The Beatles was as much a sociological movement as a musical one. The Beatles were teenagers in the staid and drab 1950s, singing to fans who came of age in the turbulent 1960s. The Beatles grew up as rebels, but wholesome, hopeful rebels. Young people, rejecting parental restrictions, were drawn to The Beatles, who brought the best of the Presley-Crickets-Jerry Lee Lewis style to creative black blues and soul. The combined ingredients of a rebellious attitude and an ingenious talent proved a recipe for success.

The Beatles worked diligently to garner the adulation of their fan base. At each step on their road to success, they pushed farther ahead on their musical journey. Working day and night over the first few years was, as Ringo so aptly put it, a hard day's night.

* * *

Patrick Crosgrove (architect) recalls a girl in Stockton California, when he was in high school. *"She was determined to get The Beatles to come to our school. She was crazy, but she was very serious about doing it."* He smiles, *"Never happened, but it was fun to talk about."*

Marcia Marcoux (author's sister-in-law): *"I can't remember too much of The Beatles' era (memory stinks!), but I do remember that my parents wouldn't let me skip CCD (religious ed) to stay home and watch the Ed Sullivan show. No VCRs back then to record."*

Ann Lees (physician): *"In the decade of the '60s I was working flat out raising 4 kids—born in 1963, 1965, 1967, 1969—with a full-time job thrown into the mix for part of the time—so I wasn't tuned in to the popular music scene, or a lot of other things of interest.*

"I first became aware of the Beatles phenomenon when Sesame Street appeared in 1968 or '69, and they played "Yellow Submarine." Both the kids and I loved that song. Later, I was very aware and shocked at the killing of John

Lennon. Still later, I had my first real introduction to the full Beatles repertoire when the CD, 1 came out around 2000. Suddenly I became a big Beatles fan, not for all their songs, but for many. Now I have several CDs, plus a big coffee-table book that also came out in the early 2000s.

"They stand so far above current popular music—no mayhem and ugly words—just fun and sometimes thoughtful lyrics—well, with a few psychedelic drugs thrown in occasionally, but no serious harm done."

Chapter Three: *Hard Day's Night*— July 10, 1964
US release—United Artists Movie Soundtrack—June 26, 1964

In the summer of 1964 I am about to enter my senior year in high school. I set up my own lawn-mowing business, charging customers one dollar for an hour of my efforts. I run for treasurer of my class and win against three girls, splitting their vote. I plan to go to Boston University after graduation. Through all the excitement of senior year I am very shy, unable to hold a conversation with a member of the opposite sex, withdrawn, and self-conscious, feeling everyone is staring at me.

And I find consolation and understanding in the songs of The Beatles, which echo in the recesses of my mind.

Politically, American youth was in search of a new symbol, a new identity. The assassination of President John F. Kennedy was a signal moment in the lives of all Americans. For the young, who had never known a prominent person's public death, Kennedy's assassination shattered their hopes and dreams. Kennedy was the symbol of youth. His New Frontier had caught on. Kennedy promised movement, and a radical repudiation of the stagnant Eisenhower years. He had the young in fold, whether serving in the

Peace Corps or the race to the moon. When Kennedy was killed at the tender age of 46, many young people lost a part of themselves.

The death of Kennedy can be seen as the ignition for an anti-establishment view, the turned-off generation, the hippie, and the radical. The vacuum allowed, indeed encouraged, the invitation of The Beatles to America. The Beatles offered an exciting distraction and a new sense of hope to a troubled people. The young generation listened longingly to the love songs of The Beatles, hoping to recreate the aura of Kennedy's Camelot.

Frank Sinatra's crooning was passé. The swinging hips and slick hairdo of Elvis Presley set the stage but were no longer new. Black musicians struggled for recognition. It was the fresh, foreign, funny Beatles who stood poised, eyes focused on America, in early 1964.

Brian Epstein carefully planned The Beatles' assault on America. He made a deal with Ed Sullivan for The Beatles to perform three live concerts in February 1964, for the princely sum of $10,000. A spot on the Ed Sullivan show ensured a television audience of millions. Convincing Capitol Records to invest $50,000 in promotional publicity was a shrewd business deal, which resulted in thousands of posters proclaiming, "The Beatles are coming."

Beatlemania surged across the Atlantic and into American homes. Boys let their hair grow longer. Girls developed a fascination for the Liverpool lads. The Beatles promoted a healthy disdain for established social mores, which delighted teenage angst, and furthered the natural rebellion against parental mores. The generation gap of the sixties had been forged.

Young people bought Beatle singles as if they were a limited edition. The Beatles dominated the music charts. They proved much more popular than the coonskin caps and hula-hoops which had been the rage of the 1950s.

Skeptics predicted The Beatles' rapid demise.

Brian Epstein wanted to conquer America, and "She Loves You" had not yet caught on in the States. He believed The Beatles needed a new commercially acceptable song to audition before the audience in the States. John and Paul got together in the basement of Jane Asher's parents' house and wrote "I Want to Hold Your Hand." Brian Epstein got his wish, and The Beatles conquered America.

The Beatles wrote, recorded, and released "I Want to Hold Your Hand," and it became their first number-one hit in the States. "I Want to Hold Your Hand" had a fast, loud, beat, and expressed the naiveté of first love. It was released on November 29, 1963, made number one on December 14, and stayed at the top of the pops for five weeks. In Great Britain it was the first time a group replaced itself at the top of the chart. It knocked "She Loves You" out of first place.

When "I Want to Hold Your Hand" was released in the States in February 1964, it was selling at the rate of 10,000 copies an hour in New York City and stayed at the top for seven weeks.

(It proved to be the first of twenty songs in six years, which were number one hits on the Billboard charts, written and recorded by The Beatles. Only in 2008 did Mariah Carey approach that landmark with eighteen top singles.)

Critics felt The Beatles were foisted on a gullible American audience by disc jockeys, led by New York's Murray the K, who promoted and publicized The Beatles, even announcing the time in Beatle minutes. Some said The Beatles were manipulated by Brian Epstein, rather than having achieved the adulation on their own. Regardless, once The Beatles landed in New York's LaGuardia Airport, greeted by thousands of screaming fans, and made their way to the Plaza Hotel on Central Park, their success in America was assured.

Elvis Presley sent them a congratulatory telegram for their appearance on the Ed Sullivan Show. The Beatles had arrived.

The invasion of America was augmented by two concerts at

Carnegie Hall on Lincoln's birthday, February 12, 1964. The enthusiastic reception by America was beyond comprehension for The Beatles. Record sales took off.

"Can't Buy Me Love" pointedly addressed the realization that there is more to life than money. The Beatles used the formula of a love song to amplify their message on broader aspects of life. With a loud, catchy beat, the tune carried itself.

The flip side of the single was Lennon's tribute to Wilson Pickett in a song entitled, "You Can't Do That." Its roughness fit well with the hard-hitting lines of "Can't Buy Me Love." The professional song-writing talent of Lennon and McCartney exhibited a fresh approach to rock and roll. John and Paul could write different songs on the same subject and match them perfectly.

By April 4, 1964, The Beatles held the top five slots in popular songs, a feat never achieved before. Or since. Number one was "Can't Buy Me Love," followed by "Twist and Shout," "She Loves You," "I Want to Hold Your Hand" and "Please Please Me." Seven more songs by The Beatles placed in the top one hundred. At the same time, *The Beatles' Second Album* eclipsed *Meet The Beatles*: the first time an artist had replaced itself with a top selling album in the States. The Beatles dominated American music.

Following their triumphant visit to the States in February 1964, The Beatles journeyed to Holland, Hong Kong, and Australia. Touring promoted their songs. Hysteria of enraptured fans accompanied their every move. Beatle wigs, Beatle lunchboxes, and Beatle magazines were everywhere. Irving Robbins created Beatle Nut ice cream in his Baskin-Robbins shops in honor of The Beatles. Beatlemania encircled the globe.

The Beatles returned to the States in the summer of 1964. On this trip Bob Dylan paid them a personal visit and introduced them to marijuana. The adulation of screaming fans was as impressive as their record record sales. In live concerts, The Beatles plucked the heartstrings of millions of teenagers. The electric atmosphere of enthusiastic fans comes through on the live recording of the Hollywood Bowl concert in August of 1964. Producer George Martin commented, "Those of us who were lucky enough to be present at a live Beatle concert will know it was not just the voice of The Beatles; it was the expression of the young people of the world."

The Beatles dominated American pop music. One song after another climbed up the music charts, as The Beatles overwhelmed other groups and shaped the future of pop music. With their single record releases, The Beatles reigned supreme.

Their singles were compiled into long playing records, but British versions did not match American lps. In England, Parlophone released two Beatle albums in 1963: *Please Please Me* and *With the Beatles*. Capitol, the American company affiliated with EMI, used a different song list in *Meet The Beatles*, the album that had so successfully spurred single sales with its debut on January 20, 1964, just as The Beatles invaded America.

Extended Play (EP) records, produced in England, had two songs on each side. When these were compiled on albums, the song lists on one side of the Atlantic did not match those on the other. Obtaining the British version of an early Beatle album was a rare coup for an American teen in the early 1960s. Regardless, Beatle albums sold no matter which songs were on them. The albums were well-packaged, professional, popular productions.

In the midst of all the fanfare, John Lennon published a collection of poems and short stories entitled, *In His Own Write*, short essays composed in the style of Edward Lear and Lewis Carroll. Lennon loved nonsense verse, abstracting the truth and mocking people with biting humor. Not only a popular singer, Lennon was capable of introducing his offbeat intellect to the literary field.

Capitol released an album entitled *Something New* in America in the summer of 1964, which featured nothing new but the song "I Want to Hold Your Hand," sung in German. The Beatles had come full circle, from singing English songs in Germany in 1961, to recording their premier love song, sung in German, three years later.

From the simplicity of their love songs of 1964, The Beatles added a satiric mockery of themselves, their fans, and the fawning press with the movie *A Hard Day's Night*, a conundrum in itself. The movie included taunts at society while recounting the days of the frenetic lives of The Beatles.

The humor of the movie was light, but telling:

Reporter: "What do you call your hairstyle?"
Ringo: "Arthur."

But there was more than mockery on screen. Timid hints of doubt crept into their most popular love ditties. Early on, The Beatles realized they had no choice but to isolate themselves from their fans; they cloaked their emotional need for separation in the popular medium of a love song. In "I'll Cry Instead" The Beatles sang of shyness when people stare at them, and how they don't know what to say. Their desire was to run away and hide, but coyly they included the option they would be back.

Like many Beatle songs, "I'll Cry Instead" can be taken on two levels. One is boy-meets-girl, and then suffers typical teenage angst. On another level, The Beatles could exploit and reveal inner fears and awe at themselves—they did not feel worthy of all the adulation and attention heaped on them.

Lennon dominated the song-writing aspects of *A Hard Day's Night*, composing the majority of the thirteen songs. McCartney contributed "And I Love Her," his first popular ballad.

For the most part, *A Hard Day's Night* continued the buoyant hope of earlier Beatle tunes. The song, itself, "A Hard Day's Night," has an interesting history. While The Beatles were busy filming the movie, the producer came to Lennon late one evening and asked for the title tune. It had not yet been written.

Next morning the producer was summoned to Lennon's dressing room. John and Paul regaled him with what turned out to be the hit song of the movie. It had, indeed, been a hard day's night, one of Ringo's malapropisms.

The movie, album, and the single of *A Hard Day's Night* proved a most successful commercial venture. It was The Beatles' first movie. It was a good, if not great soundtrack. It was a catchy, personal, number-one song.

The movie recreated the lives of The Beatles, dashing from recording studio to concert stage, with fans chasing and cheering, and the press trailing behind. The movie promoted Beatlemania. This pseudo-documentary became a success for director Richard Lester, and firmly secured The Beatles at the top of the pop world.

* * *

Al Mahoney (web designer): Al's older brother had the basement room in their house. He brought Al downstairs one day, closed the door and put on *Meet The Beatles*. Al remembers that experience to this day. Plus, he still has the album!

Peter Simon (photographer): At the age of seventeen Simon snuck his camera into Shea Stadium and caught The Beatles in action, way back when. He feels this is a good time in life to reflect on youthful memories of those glory days. Who knows where we'll all be in another twenty years?

Richard Paradise (Director, Martha's Vineyard Film Society): *"Being a huge Beatles fan and owning all their albums, I had huge expectations about the covers of the songs in* **Across the Universe***, Julie Taymor's homage to The Beatles. Thirty-three songs in all, the movie's soundtrack is a nostalgic look back to the '60s and '70s. To my delight, the covers of the songs are actually really good! Now don't get me wrong, the original Beatles songs will always be the best versions—appreciate the artistic mind of the director in their use.*

"One of my favorite scenes was the 'I've Just Seen a Face' bowling-alley scene. So creative and fun! Eddie Izzard's scene as Mr. Kite is hilarious! Also Bono's scene singing, 'I Am the Walrus, is great. Any Beatles fan will appreciate all the jokes that were thrown in there. Even if you're not a hardcore Beatles fan, you will appreciate the fantastic story, music and creative staging on screen."

Chapter Four: *Beatles for Sale*— December 4, 1964

US release—Beatles '65 December 15, 1964
and Beatles VI—June 14, 1965

Senior year in high school I drive my old '47 Plymouth into the Craft Center in Worcester, Massachusetts, to learn to make furniture. I listen to "Eight Days a Week" every time I turn on the radio. That song is symbolic of my senior year in high school: I am always busy, going from one project or activity to another, with the chess club, treasurer responsibilities, the senior play and the prom, plus the myriad of activities preparing for college.

And in that halcyon era, I am editor of our little monthly neighborhood newspaper. Friend and family gather one weekend a month and publish the Springdale News, Holden's Oldest Newspaper. From the age of 11 to 18 I continue to edit this little enterprise.

The words of "I Don't Want to Spoil the Party" and "We Can Work It Out" linger in my mind. Catchy songs by The Beatles are still with me.

Late in 1964 The Beatles released their next album, *Beatles for Sale*, which in the States, with different song lists, became *Beatles '65*. The tone of the album touched gently on themes of sorrow, anger, and dismay. Only "I Feel Fine" continued the happy, carefree, love song of earlier days. A number of tunes recount complaints of broken love and jealousy. A sense of disillusion seeped into the idyllic songs of The Beatles.

"She's a Woman" is a long way from "She Loves You." It's as if The Beatles had outgrown their innocence and faced a relationship as an adult rather than a flirtatious teenager.

The singer bemoans his lover because she no longer gives him tokens of her love. He feels disillusioned with life and love. His friends tell him she's not serious about him, and he wonders.

Questioning began. The Beatles hinted that perhaps the love affair was not working, that maybe there should be a change. Mournful pleading indicated The Beatles had a deep sense of doubt in the relationship, that their own lives were not exactly what they wanted. That doubt began to work its way into the lives of Beatle fans. As teenagers matured, they felt their own lives were not as sure and secure as before. It was time to face some hard questions.

Beatle songs evolved on a more sophisticated plane. Two songs from December 1964 bore that mature perspective. "No Reply" was the first time they told a story in a song. John Lennon took the credit for a song about visiting his girlfriend. When he saw her peek out the window, he felt sure she was with someone else. Doubt, disillusion, and dismay proved the order of the day in this song.

(Later Lennon used a similar narrative mechanism in "Norwegian Wood:" a complete story in song, with a poignant, wistful message about a tormented romance.)

"I'm a Loser" reflects another twinge of self-doubt. The singer frets over the frivolity of fame, and wonders whether he deserves such adulation. He is not the person he seems to be. He may appear happy and carefree, but actually he is pretty upset inside. In a self-analytic point, the singer recognizes the pride he feels precedes a fall from grace. In other words, don't get too cocky in love or in fame and fortune. Again, this song can be taken two ways, as a personal love song or as a reflective perspective on being a Beatle.

The Beatles began to doubt their success. They realized they had been propelled into positions of prominence by the adulation of their fans and the media. They smiled for the publicity shots but felt anguished by the forces of fame.

For their next album in the States, Capitol Records chose the original title of *Beatles VI*. The album reverted to the light and lively love songs, although a modicum of moroseness lingered from *Beatles '65*. Disappointment over a failed love affair is evident in "I Don't Want to Spoil the Party." Self-pity comes through in "What You're Doing." Sad memories prevail in "Yes It Is."

Pride was exuded in their little woman on "Every Little Thing." Not having enough time for love was the theme of "Eight Days a Week." The contrast of dismay and anger versus pride and joy was explored in the context of a love song. Several tunes brought out the lively beat, which makes the songs memorable, decades after they topped the pop charts.

Ever-present optimism emerged in "Tell Me What You See." No matter how bleak a lover may feel, there is hope everything will work out. I'll make your life so much better, the singer pleads, if only you stay with me. The element of trust plays a poignant part in this love song.

Beatles VI proved the final chapter in the book of Beatlemania in the sense that it was an album comprised solely of love songs. The Beatles' first six albums contain enough love songs to last a lifetime. They met the needs of their audience, enduring the personal pain and pangs of adolescence, still full of innocence. Through their love songs, The Beatles conveyed an optimistic message and shared honest emotions about love.

In affairs of the heart, The Beatles drew on personal experience. The press was quick to link any Beatle to a favorite girl. Fans were just as eager to try to claim one of the moptops for their own. When they sang in nightclubs in Liverpool and later in Hamburg, there was always competition to win a Beatle heart. The Beatles enjoyed the fanfare but did not take it seriously. They were in their early twenties and more intent on making it in music, than with a girl, though girls were never far from their hearts and minds.

In lettering class in art school Cynthia Powell sat behind John Lennon and became his girlfriend. The two were inseparable, except when the opportunity arose to go to Hamburg. That's when John learned to write sweet nothings in his love letters.

When Cynthia learned she was pregnant, they got married, on August 22, 1962. Brian Epstein feared fan resentment, and decreed they keep the marriage secret. The image that The Beatles were all young bachelors with bounding good looks, charm, and sexuality, was promulgated far and wide. And it was that image that captured America and contributed to fan hysteria. Lennon kept his marriage, like his poor eyesight, a secret, until it became impossible to conceal, either with his wire-rim glasses or the birth of Julian Lennon.

Rumors surfaced that the other Beatles were involved with women. Ringo Starr married his girlfriend from Liverpool, Maureen Cox, in February 1965, and George Harrison met Patti Boyd on the set of *A Hard Day's Night* and married her in January 1966. Paul remained the elusive bachelor, though he had girlfriends, from Dot Spencer, who followed him to Hamburg, to Jane Asher, an aspiring actress who spurned marriage for an acting career, then became a popular, talented cake baker.

* * *

Many Beatle songs from 1965 stand on their own as autobiographical essays or social critiques. The Beatles wrote about their lives and experiences around them. "Dr. Robert" and

"Paperback Writer" were social commentaries, cloaked in a safe satiric song so critics couldn't challenge the conceit. Each song bore a message that all was not right with the world. The Beatles realized they could use their prominent public podium to make sly social commentary.

An example of the tyranny of life was retold in "We Can Work It Out," a song that implies compromise, cooperation, and communication, but has a selfish, macho undertone. The song presents a fellow arguing with his girl friend, trying to persuade her to change his mind. The message is simple: let's compromise, but if you don't do it my way, we're through. The simplicity of the song is that the persona is speaking from the viewpoint that he is absolutely right, and will tolerate no criticism or argument. The Beatles satirize this self-centered outlook on life.

In recognition of their popularity, or perhaps in response to the enormous commercial success The Beatles brought to England, Queen Elizabeth bestowed a major honor on them when she named them to be Members of the British Empire in June of 1965.

The Beatles accepted the honor in character, joking with the royal family and thoroughly enjoying themselves at the ceremony, nervous though they may have been. Rumor has it they calmed down by smoking a joint in the men's room of Buckingham Palace before they were ushered in before Her Majesty.

Some stuffy old conservatives were outraged at the Queen for granting The Beatles the award, and one MBE turned in his medal. John Lennon's question put the uproar in perspective: "What's going to hold up his pajamas?" The MBE awards spurred The Beatles on to greater efforts, which resulted in a prolific outpouring of popular songs.

Two tunes released in mid-1965 show the disdain The Beatles felt toward the girl who got away. "Ticket to Ride" was their first venture into heavy metal, and the first Beatle song more than three minutes long. Lennon's haughty anger is evident. His girl doesn't care about him any more and she's going to leave him. He gives permission for her to go, if that's what she wants. His attitude is, "take me as I am or leave."

Another reading on the tune is that the song refers to a railway ticket to Ryde, which is on the Isle of Wight, where McCartney had a cousin who tended bar. The Beatles pushed the envelope with double meanings wherever possible.

Later that year, 1965, The Beatles perfected the description of the girl who got away in "Daytripper," a rough, raw, rock song that contained the theme of broken love. "Daytripper" also refers to a drug trip, and is a reference to (infrequently) dropping acid; not a serious user, but someone who only does drugs when they get the chance, a weekend druggie.

The Beatles evolved. As a unique group, they justifiably earned stardom and fame. Concert managers and record producers needed a star, and The Beatles filled that role admirably. Popularity gave them the opportunity to push rock and roll to new limits. They were at once an example of self-striving, Liverpool lads striving for success, but morphed into stars, suited to meet the public's demand.

The Beatles disparaged the very media that helped hype them to limitless success. The Beatles reflected the society that produced them. The message songs they began to write in 1965 were similar to Dylan's songs. But The Beatles, under the tutelage of George Martin, used their studio palette to perfect their style and create esthetically pleasing melodies, in sharp contrast to the ragged, loose, unfinished songs Dylan was known for. Beatle tunes were characterized by completion, perfection, and exactitude.

The Beatles evolved into a group of young men who masterfully handled the mantle of great expectations thrust upon them. No longer content solely to serve the role their fans sought; they rose to a level of serious social commentary. They relished the challenge, the change, and the chance to forge a new direction in rock music. Not content to stand still, they sought new songs to mimic and imitate. Beatle music was neither static nor decadent. They pushed the boundaries of the studio and of their own creativity. Each new Beatle song was fresh, alive, and a vibrant piece of music, intellectually pleasing, musically ear catching, and stood on its own. There was no Beatle sound; it was Beatle music, which, by definition, was unique. And yet because of their popularity, there is a familiarity whenever one hears a song The Beatles wrote.

During the six years The Beatles reigned supreme, from 1964 to 1969, they wrote and recorded forty-seven popular songs, far more than their nearest contemporary competitor, the Temptations. Those 47 hits were concentrated mostly in the early years, because The Beatles wrote, recorded, and released a new song every few weeks. As they matured, and spent more time in the studio, it took longer to meet their own stringent standards. They worked to complete an album theme, rather than produce a collection of songs. So, although it was their earlier work that led to major sales records and created the exuberance of Beatlemania, their later work was more refined, experimental, and intellectually challenging.

Did fans buy Beatle songs because The Beatles composed them or because the songs themselves were catchy, unique and different? To prove a point, Paul McCartney wrote songs for his girlfriend's brother, Peter Asher, of Peter and Gordon. With most of the songs Paul used his own name, but on one song, "Woman," he used the pseudonym Bernard Webb, to see what would happen. Amazingly, the song raced up the charts, and people asked who was this unknown composer, Webb, who writes so well! It seemed The Beatles could do no wrong.

In part, The Beatles stayed at the top because other bands did not have the breaks nor the talent that landed in The Beatles' laps. How could the Dave Clark Five or Herman's Hermits compete with the compositions of Lennon and McCartney? What parent would allow their teen to witness the antics of The Who or The Rolling Stones, when The Beatles offered a fresher, cleaner take to rock and roll? Who could manage a group the way Brian Epstein did? Who had the technical and production skills of a George Martin? To be sure, there was a bandwagon effect. Because of The Beatles' popularity, more people knew of them, which contributed to more record sales. Success bred success as The Beatles built on their reputation and continued to knock out hit songs.

And yet, The Beatles became captives of their own success. The wild hysteria associated with their concerts and public appearances propelled them out of their lower-class backgrounds and thrust them into celebrity status, but caused them to pause and wonder what had happened to them and where they were going.

Their love songs were on the verge of becoming repetitive riffs. Should they continue to sing redundant romantic ruminations or could they define a new identity in pop music? What did their audience seek in mid-1965? Where was the American youth movement headed? Could The Beatles retain their spot at the top of the pops? Were they destined to be prisoners of their pop music image, or could they forge a new focus with their music?

The Beatles cried out for Help!

* * *

Susan Desmaris (social worker): *"My first 45 was 'Daytripper,' and I played it so much I thought my parents would kill me. I can't even remember what the flip side was, but I remember 'Daytripper.'"* (It was "We Can Work It Out")

Holly Nadler (author): *"I was a Rolling Stones fan back then. The Beatles were not cool enough for me. But now I listen to their songs, and they are* *so intricate, so well done, they mean much more to me. And my son Charlie put together an iPod selection of Beatle songs when we drove out to California, and it was the sweetest thing he ever did. I just loved listening to The Beatles."*

Josephine Truesdell (teacher): *"[My brothers] Jock and Frank bought me my very first album. It was* **Meet the Beatles**, *of course! Below are a couple of paragraphs from my Dylan talk that have to do with The Beatles. The year is 1964:*

"That winter and spring Dylan toured a lot, both in the states as well as in Europe. During intermission at one of his concerts in London he received a telegram from John Lennon, saying how sorry all The Beatles were not to be able to be there that night. Dylan had not yet met The Beatles—he had not been that taken with their songs, in fact...like 'I Want to Hold Your Hand,' they were a bit too teeny-boppery for his taste, a bit too similar to all those "silly little love songs"—but The Beatles had apparently been quite taken with Dylan's songs, playing his **Freewheelin'** *album until it had worn out its grooves...and shortly he would become very good friends with the foursome, particularly with John Lennon and George Harrison.*

"Not long after Newport, Dylan finally had the opportunity to 'Meet The Beatles' (that was the title of my very first album!) in New York. He attended their concert at the Paramount Theater, and noted a major difference between their concerts and his: when The Beatles played, it was pandemonium throughout; when he played, the audience hung onto his every word, waiting until the very end to applaud. (Dylan was quite proud of that, of course...the words he penned were important to him, and were the true essence of his songs.) The Fab Four and the boy from Minnesota got together that night and, as Sounes writes, neither Dylan's nor The Beatles' music would ever be the same after that meeting: Bob began integrating Beatles-like use of rock and roll into his music, and The Beatles began to write lyrics that had the depth and seriousness of Dylan's songs. John Lennon notes that songs such as The Beatles' hits, 'I'm a Loser' and 'You've Got to Hide Your Love Away,' are from his "Dylan Period." In the book **Bob Dylan: Intimate Insights from Friends**

and Fellow Musicians, *Lennon said [Prior to meeting Bob Dylan], 'I'd have a separate songwriting John Lennon who wrote songs for the meat market, and I didn't consider them to have any depth at all. [After meeting Bob Dylan] I started being me about the songs [no longer] writing them objectively, but subjectively.'*

"And, Joe Klein explains Dylan's own evolution after his meeting with The Beatles in his biography of Woody Guthrie: 'Bob Dylan wasn't a folklorist [like Woody Guthrie], [solely] dedicated to preserving and promoting a beloved tradition...nor was he a singing political organizer like [Pete] Seeger. He didn't disdain popular music [as they did]—Elvis Presley had been his first hero. He'd chosen folk music because, at the time, it offered [him] more creative freedom than rock and roll. But, all the old formulas had been washed away with the arrival of The Beatles'...and that is when Dylan began to spend his time quietly experimenting with rock musicians—an abomination to many in the folk world at the time, and soon to cause a major mark in the annals of popular music."

Chapter Five: *Help!*—August 6, 1965

"Help!" grabs me. Graduation from high school precipitates doubts and fears about the future. Had I grown up too fast? Would I make it in college? What lies ahead? The words to "Help!" are so specific as to speak directly to me and to everyone who listens closely. It is a powerfully personal song.

Even as The Beatles underwent their public identity crisis, I undergo an emotional break with my past. The leap from the security of high school to the anticipation of college is one of the major shifts in growing up. Not everyone makes the transition smoothly, and the doubts associated with the change in status are legion. As I set off for college in the fall of 1965, fears and opportunities boggle my mind, and I look to The Beatles for Help!

The Beatles underwent a public identity crisis in 1965 with the release of the single-album-movie *Help!* The album *Help!* was released in the United Kingdom on August 6, 1965. The album contained seven songs from the movie soundtrack, and seven more original tunes, including the most recorded song in The Beatles repertoire, "Yesterday." "Ticket to Ride" and "Help!" were also big singles on both sides of the Atlantic.

The hit song, "Help!" was a musical metaphor, ripe with despair and disillusion. The Beatles saw themselves in an uncomfortable new light. Fame proved distasteful. Their minds were in turmoil. They had accomplished too much too fast, yet wanted even more.

John Lennon penned the memorable lines for "Help!" in a searing, pained, autobiographic rendition, bemoaning a youth that passed too fast. Lennon recognized his zeal for independence, but now that he was grown up—he was almost 25 when he wrote this song—he realized he had changed, which proved both frightening and depressing. His insecurity was evident, and he couched his doubts in the patented love song, as he sought solace from his girlfriend to ease his pain.

It's a powerful piece. "Help!" bares his soul as Lennon exposes his vulnerability. Initially Lennon sought to sing the song at a slower pace, like Roy Orbison's "Only the Lonely." Lennon was distraught and overwhelmed by the success of The Beatles and later referred to this era as his "fat Elvis" period. The song revealed his inner doubts and fears, a dramatic example of his public persona.

With this single song, The Beatles took a giant step forward. They left behind the simple love ditty to tackle problems of identity, self-assessment, growth, and maturity. In song, but also in their personal lives, The Beatles underwent major changes in a search, a struggle, to find out what they were all about.

In *Help!* The Beatles began a musical and literary trek that ran the gamut through the rest of their career. This single set the tone for a series of songs that dealt with the search for self and gave The Beatles the means to deal with their own identity.

No longer were they content to continue as pop heroes, raking in millions of dollars for singing simple love songs. They felt compelled to say something profound, to probe deeply into the life-shaping questions young people were asking. They sought greater accomplishments, both musically and verbally, yet still in the context of a love song, their established forte.

It is intriguing that the flip side of the single "Help!" was titled,

"I'm Down," which described the dismay of a lover who discovers his woman isn't everything he wanted her to be. A sense of loneliness, conflict, and rejection meander through "I'm Down."

This disillusion with love and dismay toward life arose even as The Beatles were strapped into the roller coaster of fame and popularity, still very much on the way up, financially bringing in the cash, and enjoying the rebates of adulation from Beatlemania. Yet they felt cramped, confused, and confined and sought release and escape, a new lease on life.

As George Harrison commented on the future of The Beatles, a dozen years after the breakup: *There never was any doubt. The Beatles were doomed. Your own space, man, it's so important. That's why we were doomed, because we did not have any. We were like monkeys in a zoo. There was never anything in any of the Beatle experiences really that good. Even the best thrill soon got tiring.*

The price of fame and money is pride, and pride precedes a downfall. The Beatles' doubts were internal, yet they externalized their fears, and the public sympathized with their dilemma, even as they continued to idolize the group. Critics predicted the imminent collapse of The Beatles, even as The Beatles wondered in song what made them so special. The mood of simple love songs, evident in the first Beatle albums, underwent a subtle change to introduce a hint of dismay and sorrow, culminating in the display of dissatisfaction and self-deception, characterized by "Help!" and its B-side echo, "I'm Down."

While the movie *Help!* did not match the creativity, spontaneity, and novelty of *A Hard Day's Night*, the songs were just as popular. The Beatles sang about problems of growing up, an effort to explore what it means to find out who you are and what you want to be. Questions of childhood dreams, parental authority, security, and independence were at issue. American youth were in a struggle with these conceits in 1965. Beatles' songs spoke to a real need in their audience.

Self-analysis, trying to find out who you want to be, and what you want to do, were topical concerns among baby-boomers coming of age in the mid-'60s. Bob Dylan originated this "message rock," but The Beatles soon proved masters in writing and singing songs aimed directly at teenagers all across America.

The songs on *Help!* bespeak loneliness in life, sorrow over arguments, and unfulfilled hopes in romance. There are expressions of doubt and fear, questions whether this is the right girl, and dismay about how to fulfill expectations.

"You've Got to Hide Your Love Away" explores these issues in a mournful manner. There's acknowledgment that the persona is unnerved when people stare at him. He feels they talk about him, behind his back. The sense of anguish is evident from the opening line about holding one's head in one's hand. Helplessness pervades the song, and the fear, as the title suggests, is that the persona has to conceal his love from the prying eyes of the public.

At the end of *Help!* we are left with the sense that The Beatles sought to distance themselves from the love-song mantra that brought them such success. Now they had something to say, but were too reserved, too angry, or too insecure to say it. They expressed that doubt in song. They felt depressed. They were embarrassed at the ease with which they had created this vast following of fans, infatuated by their love songs. What they sought now was to move forward and explore their inner feelings.

The Beatles hid their love away. Their work had progressed well beyond the simple love song. Their audience sought a new message. With the release of *Help!* in August 1965, The Beatles forever turned their back on the puppy-love songs of Beatlemania which had propelled them into the limelight in 1963. They were now intent on creating a body of work that would make a more significant contribution to the world of music.

Ringo, the eldest Beatle, had not yet turned twenty-five.

Where could they go next? What new songs could they write? What new stories would emerge? These were burning questions for fans in the mid-1960s. The Beatles already had started to move beyond the adulation of success. They grew comfortable with the fame of rock stardom but sought more in the realm of influence and dominance, an opportunity to expand and clarify their personal ideals and wishes, their philosophies of what life could and should be. The overriding theme of the love song was a constant in their scheme. And right to the end of their term, The Beatles would revert to the love song to paint their picture. But in later years they used the love song to frame deeper feelings and desires. All you need was love, but it was not that easy to find or hold on to.

The Beatles, four individuals from similar lower-middle-class backgrounds, managed to form a tight band with a united front and mature into a group of musicians capable of producing a serious love melody such as "All My Loving," or a searing attack on their own vulnerability with "Help!" Their talent knew no bounds, from songs to movies to live concerts. And it all evolved from the simplicity of a love song. The Beatles adapted the love song in a more reflective, nostalgic tone as they filed into the recording studio to produce *Rubber Soul* in the latter part of 1965.

* * *

Carl Holt (television editor) was born in 1966 so he had to grow into The Beatles. His sister had a bunch of their records, but he had to find out about The Beatles on his own. Eventually he bought all their albums, and to this day, considers himself a fan.

My daughter **Jill** wrote: *"Hi, pop—you are probably the most loyal Beatles fan ever; would make them proud. I love your essay. It's interesting to hear about the quick success of the album and The Beatles from way back when;*

interesting to think that all you baby boomers were lost twenty-somethings as well."

Irene Tewksbury (librarian): *"I was in elementary school and younger during The Beatles, and I remember more about the other album, where if you played part of it backwards it was supposed to say, 'Paul is dead.'*

"Kathy, my old boss, once got to meet The Beatles on a plane when she was in high school! They invited her and her friends on the plane and were perfect gentleman about it. They talked, and then the girls left! She was struck dumb with awe at the time!" (It turns out it was the Rolling Stones, but it was still a great experience.)

She goes on. *"When we were little, my mother would put me in the tub with my sister Susie. We'd play a splashing game, pretending to drum the water while chanting 'Ringo Starr! Ringo Starr!' My cousin memorized the German words to 'I Want to Hold your Hand' to impress us. Our teenaged sisters made sure we watched The Beatles on Ed Sullivan."*

Chapter Six: *Rubber Soul*—December 3, 1965

Christmas 1965. The Beatles have just released Rubber Soul. My two brothers, still in high school, and I each buy the album as a gift, so we end up with three copies of Rubber Soul. We spend that long-ago Christmas listening, over and over, to the nostalgic ballads of The Beatles. It is a Christmas that lingers to this day. And whenever I play the album, or even look at the cover, I smell the scent of balsam Christmas trees.

Rubber Soul means many things to me: nostalgia, sentiment, and a twist on romance. It harbors a sense of doubt and insecurity, yet contains a host of elegant musical ballads. I sense a string quartet playing in the background. "In My Life" is the music for a video I did of residents in a nursing home. "In My Life" is the name of a novel I wrote about coming of age in the 60s, facing abortion and the draft. "In My Life" is the song my daughter Amy and I danced to at her wedding. "In My Life" symbolizes the link with my past, our past. It still stands as one of the major musical pieces of the era, in my mind.

With their cries for Help! The Beatles forever changed pop music. They had reached success beyond their wildest dreams. They now sought to reexamine their values, reassess their ideals, and redirect their goals. Their intent was to better understand themselves and consequently express their feelings more appropriately to a growing legion of fans. Theirs was a very personal approach to pop music.

Beatle fans took to this new role as an example of the depth of The Beatles' awareness of the trials of life. Instead of isolating themselves behind the security of superstardom, The Beatles sought new roads to wander, challenging styles to develop, more mature feelings to evoke. Four months after *Help!* they released *Rubber Soul*, just in time for the Christmas market.

Rubber Soul. The title itself is a conundrum, a twist on the psyche and the flexibility of style. The title meant there was more than met the ear. The songs on *Rubber Soul* evoke a new type of love song: a romantic folk-ballad. The Beatles incorporated a baroque tone in their music. Looking at life and love through a more refined lens, they created a mature, artistic album. This reflected an audience who had outgrown the simplicity of love songs and now sought more meaningful tunes with sensitivity and depth.

Looking at the attitude of The Beatles we find roots for disillusion with love in the album *Rubber Soul*. There are twelve songs on the album, (fourteen on the British version), all relating to affection for a woman. One feels the sense of exuberance at first finding a girl in "I've Just Seen a Face," and the ideal love in "Michele." But a deeper review of *Rubber Soul* shows that everything is not perfect. There is a breakup between lovers, arrogance and disdain among partners, and a sense of doubt filters through the album.

Love is not secure. Arguments and disagreements ensue. These are signs The Beatles were struggling with their own image as idealists who seek to project a thoughtful realism. *Rubber Soul* represents a rebuke of the image of ideal love. From the cries of "Help!" which propelled The Beatles into a search of their own inner feelings, to the concept of an ever-changing inner-self—an elastic ego presented as a baroque love medley—The Beatles created a best-selling album of romantic ballads.

McCartney's "I'm Looking Through You" set the tone. The melancholy question, the self-doubt, the desire for the way things used to be, are all expressed in this powerful piece that says, now I see you differently. You aren't the same person as when I met you. Such statements are so true in a relationship—people change. Relationships evolve. The penetrating examination of a lover is a challenge for a young man to handle, and McCartney captured these emotions in song.

The persona questions his woman. And the woman could personify Beatle fans who did not want The Beatles to change, to grow, to evolve. The song is an attack on the nowhere people of the world. "I'm Looking Through You" expresses outrage at the public, fans who blindly followed The Beatles, wanting them to roll out the same tired tunes. But The Beatles had moved beyond Beatlemania. They wanted to be heard in a more noble light than pop-music idols, yet they framed their plaint in the conventional concerns of a romantic relationship.

This situation was akin to when Bob Dylan went electric at the Newport Folk Festival that same year of 1965. He was booed by fans who did not want him to change. They wanted him forever glued to his acoustic guitar. Now, in song, The Beatles expressed their need, their desire, and their effort to move forward.

In *Rubber Soul* there is dismay and doubt over love. "You Won't See Me" describes anger at a girl immune to the emotions her lover feels for her. After a fight, the girl leaves, and the lover is despondent that he may have lost her. She's on the phone. It's a sad place to be, and the persona offers a desperate plea to re-connect, but we know their affair is over. Since they broke up, it feels like forever. Again, The Beatles expressed the feelings and sensibilities of their teenage audience.

McCartney described his frustration with little things, so the larger issues are overlooked. The Beatles acknowledged some girls are not as great as they seem, that the ideal love is not the most honest portrayal of a love affair. In *Rubber Soul* The Beatles explored a more realistic rendition of love.

The tide turns when the woman gets the upper hand. In "Drive My Car" the girl is on her way to fame, when she hires the persona as her chauffeur. She has aspirations to be a famous movie star, and needs a driver to get her around. The power is now in the hands of the woman, and she intends to hold that over her humble driver. In this case, however, the girl doesn't have what it takes. The denouement is revealed that she has no car, but at least has a driver!

The initial title for this song was "You Can Give Me Golden Rings," but Lennon suggested using the motif of driving the car, a euphemism for sex. Thus The Beatles slyly inserted a bit of daring do in the song. Harrison played bass, with McCartney on lead guitar, a role reversal for these two.

"Michele" depicts the lover as a young man who has just found a new romance and wants to express his affection. His words are forceful and winsome and sung in French. He seeks to be accepted, but inherent is his fear of rejection. He is cautious, to the point of melancholy, as if he fears his love is too late. The lover feels incompetent, unworthy, and abashedly unable to communicate his emotions. Yet he wants her to know she means so much to him, so he speaks in French, the language of love.

From man/woman haughtiness and disdain to a pleading song of love, The Beatles cover the gamut of love songs on *Rubber Soul*. Searching, struggling, seeking, they sought new justifications for songs of love.

Even religion slipped into a love song, as "The Word" comments on the gospel as it relates to a love ballad. The word love, of course, is a constant in Beatle songs. The Beatles found religious justification in the book—the Bible—for their love songs. It is a grand statement of faith to sing about a newfound love, just as preachers proselytize about the value and virtue of love, which truly is the basis of religion. We have come full circle. If you find love, or find God, you have found everything.

The Beatles were spokesmen for a religion of love. Love is the most universal element of humanity. It binds people together, expresses beauty and hope, and describes the unity of mankind. And The Beatles continued to capture that essence in song.

"The Word" is told in autobiographic style. At first the persona was disillusioned by religion, then thought he understood it, now wants to spread the gospel. In 1965 The Beatles appreciated there was a lot of love in the Bible and the concept of God and Christianity gave backbone and foundation to their love songs.

The Beatles had a sincere but simplistic view of religion. They saw their remarkable rise to success as a result of the philosophy of love. "The Word" was John Lennon's attempt to justify The Beatles to the establishment. This was Lennon's first attempt at an anthem, a political statement that could easily be learned. There was credence in their religion of love and serious social content in *Rubber Soul*, arguably one of The Beatles' best albums.

"Girl" is a tortuous lament in the choice between money and love. It is the story of a girl who found pleasure inflicting pain on her lover. Lennon read the book, *Pain and Pleasure*, before he penned this song. The piece is plaintive and pleading, as if Lennon is trying to please this insatiable woman. Enraptured by her captivating personality, he worries about her incessant, insatiable demands.

The persona is head-over-heels in love, but his woman tortures him. He cannot leave her because she needles him and then promises him everything. She teases him, belittles him, and yet he lacks the gumption to leave. It's a powerful, pleading song of lovers who stay together, even at the cost of the pain generated by the relationship.

This sorry saga bears a potent message. We wonder if we are truly appreciated by our partner when we struggle so hard to make our lover happy. This song stands as an integral part of the evolution of Beatle thought, for it describes the dilemma of lovers who grapple with the choice between love and money or love and career or love and the rest of life. The Beatles sought more than material wealth. Financial security may appear more attractive than love, but "Wait," there's more.

Incidentally, in the chorus of "Girl," a couple of Beatles can be heard singing, "Tit, tit, tit," which is a little more risqué than the "Beep, Beep, yeah," in the background of "Drive My Car."

Sometimes one has to probe inwardly to find joy in life. The Beatles dealt with unhappiness in the world. "Wait" is a song of hope at a reunion after a spat between lovers. The persona hopes to reconcile after an awkward scene, to work it out and move on. "Wait" is a song that challenges the listener to put the sadness or anger of a disagreement behind them, to limit the heartbreak. "Even though your heart is broken, I'm coming home to make everything right once more," the persona seems to say.

The potential for reconciliation lies just beneath the surface of *Rubber Soul*. The lasting impression from the album is a sense life can be improved, but it isn't easy. Both sides must compromise and make amends; only then can the relationship be salvaged. In *Rubber Soul* there is the chance the argument will not be resolved, and we must be prepared for the consequences. No more puppy love; now the themes brim with depth and angst. The Beatles recognize the deeper qualities of life and love, of money and career, of changing emotions in a relationship. *Rubber Soul* probed deeper into the mind and soul than any previous Beatle album.

The most popular song of the *Rubber Soul* era was the tormented ballad "Yesterday," the best-known song The Beatles ever wrote. It touched more people with its tune and words and manner than virtually any other popular song. "Yesterday" ranks as one of the most popular songs of all time. Although it was included in the album *Help!*, released in the summer of 1965, it presaged the nostalgia of *Rubber Soul*, which went on the market at the end of that year.

Yet "Yesterday" was not included on either the American version of *Help!* or *Rubber Soul*. In an obvious marketing effort, Capital Records packaged the song in its own album, *Yesterday…and Today*. This album bore the infamous butcher cover, featuring The Beatles dressed in bloody white aprons, wielding meat cleavers, with broken dolls strewn across the cover. It was a tasteless choice, and immediately recalled, but not before several hundred albums were printed and sold. They quickly became collectors' prizes.

When Paul first played the tune of "Yesterday" to John, he called it "Scrambled Egg." Once he worked out the heartfelt melody, which came to him in a dream, Paul penned the words to "Yesterday." This song comes alive as the persona expresses a wealth of emotion as he contemplates life without his girlfriend. What a difference a day makes.

The angst of lost love. He had everything yesterday, but today he is bereft, lonely, and lost. Yesterday he had faith, and everything seemed perfect, but now that idyllic world is shattered. The persona wants to escape, get away, put the past behind him, but the shadow of love lingers, and he cannot shake the gloom that drapes his soul.

Yesterday, deeply in love; today, the sorrows descend on the persona. The song is simple and poignant, sad, and lonely. McCartney's melodious voice, with a soft string accompaniment, captures the essence of their Baroque era of rock music.

There is a sense the singer cannot go on with life, that because he has lost his love he cannot function. This is a novel approach to a love song: sweet and sad at once. "Yesterday" was sung in a poignant, pleading manner. The melody makes the listener sit up and listen. It is the most recorded of all the Beatle songs, with more than three thousand cover versions. It can be heard at symphony concerts or played by nightclub minstrels. A new group gains instant recognition if they do justice to their individual rendition of "Yesterday."

One can look at "Yesterday" in another vein, as a song of self-doubt, of recognition of the inadequacies and failures in life. "Yesterday" cautiously continues the theme of self examination explored in "Help!" The song reveals the sense that The Beatles are now aware of their own hypocrisy, their selves and their souls.

A second song from the English version of *Help!* didn't make it to America until *Rubber Soul* and was released, months later. Paul McCartney sang with exuberance on "I've Just Seen a Face," but there is a hint of doubt at the chance he might have lost his girl. The element of chance does play a role in love. Once we meet a lover, we wonder what would have happened had we never met. What if I walked down a different street, tarried longer over morning coffee, rode the bus instead of walking.

In many ways, "I've Just Seen a Face" is a mirror image of "Yesterday," as this song looks forward with hope and optimism, rather than backward with regret. The element of chance gives this song an upbeat mood, rather than the somber sense conjured in "Yesterday."

Total commitment and infatuation are registered in this encounter with a new love, even planning to dream about her. The joy at finding the right woman, so unique and different, makes some people keep falling in love, over and over again.

McCartney let loose with a romper in "Got to Get You into My Life." It is loud, fast, with a catchy rhythm, and has withstood the test of time. The pounding beat and piercing vocals remind one of

McCartney's version of "Long Tall Sally." It's rock and roll played and sung to the hilt.

Again, it is a song about chance. The persona may have had a different reaction had he taken a different route. Life could be so different. This mimes Robert Frost and "The Road Not Taken," but gives rise to the excuse that if I keep looking, keep putting myself out there, I'll find the person who's perfect for me.

(In McCartney's own life, he and Linda Eastman were married thirty years, in a loving, caring relationship. When Sir Paul sought a new love, after Linda's death, his matrimonial tenure was less than three years, and cost him nearly fifty million dollars when he divorced Heather Mills in 2008.)

"Norwegian Wood" recounted a mystical adventure in love. John Lennon told the story of girl who took advantage of him, a woman with unclear motives. At the time he wrote the song, it was rumored John was having an affair and disguised it in song so his wife would not find out. The plaintive voice is filled with angst at his sorrowful romance, about a girl he felt took advantage of him.

The fabric of the tale unravels as John explains how he was invited to the girl's house, where he had to sit on the floor, as there was not a chair. They talked for a while, and then she went to bed, leaving Lennon, to sleep in the bathtub. In the morning, she left him. The subtitle, "This Bird Had Flown," aptly summarizes Lennon's tale of woe, and a subtle reference to marijuana is contained in the words, Norwegian Wood, a joint.

Lennon's song "Run for Your Life" displays an arrogance and disdain for women. This may be a macho song carried to the extreme, but it is so harsh as to be almost satirical. The anger and jealousy expressed in song bespeaks an arrogance which Lennon admittedly felt in his youth, and which Yoko Ono worked so hard to re-direct.

John Lennon recalled he treated girls with a haughty arrogance as a teenager. This song is harsh, rough, and honest, and probably reveals more about male/female relations than The Beatles actually wanted. Lennon later admitted it was one song he seriously regretted writing, yet it was Harrison's favorite tune on *Rubber Soul*.

George Harrison chose a different way to express himself in love. He saw it as a lost and lonely experience. Harrison's songs were dreamy, subjective statements welded together in musical unity and presented as thoughts, rather than completed deeds. We clearly know how Lennon and McCartney were foiled in romance; we seldom learn what happened to Harrison in his wayward twists and trysts.

Harrison expressed his feelings more dramatically than he described his actions. From anger and loneliness over losing one's love, there comes a period of doubt and question. Like Lennon's *Run for Your Life*, Harrison put down his woman in a song entitled *Think for Yourself*, a defiant request for his woman to take control of herself.

Anger at the girlfriend's lies upset the singer. He wants her to do her own thing, and not to bother him. Do it your way, and leave me out of it. He says he has moved beyond her, that she is too caught up in herself and makes him unhappy. He asks her to be more sensible. He offers hope, and gives her time, but returns to his initial statement that she's got to do it herself.

Although the song is laden with clichés, it rings true. Harrison makes his point succinctly: I've moved on; it's time for you to get over it. Harrison came into his own as a songwriter with "Think for Yourself." It secured his reputation for biting statements against people he didn't respect. His harsh ballad minces no words.

Lennon and McCartney rarely plumbed the depth of antagonism, personal commitment, and involvement that Harrison found in song. Harrison delved into the deeper recesses of the mind, although he never matched the other two as an accomplished lyrical songmaster.

Rubber Soul. An album title with a pliable intent, a collection of songs that dealt with an ambiguous study of relationships in life and love. *Rubber Soul* was the first studio attempt by The Beatles to escape the road-show atmosphere. It was an effort to move in a different direction, almost folk, but a retreat from message rock. *Rubber Soul* marked a significant turning point in the evolution, the maturation, of The Beatles.

Even as they challenged their fans with music heading in a new direction, The Beatles looked back from how far they had come. They expressed nostalgia for their past, for the carefree days of their youth, for the friends who helped their climb to the top. Sentiments are scattered through Beatle songs, but emerge most vividly with "In My Life," a masterpiece of reflection and appreciation for lost youth. "In My Life" is a poignant thank you to the people and places of The Beatles' past, and it resonates over time with its poignant expression of gratitude. John Lennon's poetry is both romantic and evocative as he reminisces on his past.

Places in our lives have changed, as have the people of our past. The singer recalls the influential friends and family who went before, and conjures up a love for them in his heart. The poignancy of this song lingers decades after the tune fades. Lennon captured a nostalgia for youth that is virtually universal in human behavior. It is an amazing song for a twenty-five-year-old poet to compose.

With "In My Life" Lennon touched more people than he ever imagined in that song. He made his mark with his music, and that single song resonates decades later. Fans still take the time to "stop and think about him."

"In My Life" characterizes *Rubber Soul.* It fits the Baroque tenor of the album with a nostalgic love ballad, but it is more than just a song. It is a statement by a young poet who reflected on his past. It is a tribute to lost youth, to friends and lovers who helped along the way, an especially tender rendition for pop music. It evokes classic sentiment and thus links rock and roll to a musical past. In style and substance, the song "In My Life" has come to epitomize the album *Rubber Soul*.

Even as The Beatles looked backward, they moved ahead. They surged forward beyond *Rubber Soul* with another unique album, *Revolver*, which dared to head in a very different direction, and went round and round and round, turning like a record album on the turntable.

* * *

Pat Kelley (teacher): *"Of course I remember the night The Beatles were on Ed Sullivan. I was in parochial school, and the boys couldn't let their hair grow long, like The Beatles. And the night John Lennon was shot. That was so horrible."*

Eric Alexander : *"The Beatles were the only group for whom parents would bring their children to buy their records. Now it's grandparents who bring their grandchildren to listen to their records."*

Carol Carrick (author): *"It was the only music my kids and I could listen to together. No other music brings kids and parents together."*

Cindy Kurth (singer) recalls that Beatle songs helped her through both good times and bad. After a long week at school, she and a friend would celebrate with "Beatle nights" consisting solely of listening to the Beatles or watching their movies. Beatle nights were one of her favorite memories with friends.

Amy Dresser Held (administrator/educator/daughter):
"Hey dad, I have lots of memories of being a kid and belting out beatles songs inside one of your VW Rabbits— 'Yellow Submarine,' 'Hard Days Night'… my favorite Beatles song is 'In My Life' that we danced together to at my wedding—the lyrics and music are so beautiful and make me cry every time— a song about true lasting love."

Chapter Seven: *Revolver*—August 5, 1966

That first year at Boston University, in the Division of General Education, spurs me to academic achievement and physical challenges. I thrill at links between literature and ancient history. I thrive in the academic atmosphere as one epiphany after another amazes me. And I blossom in the glow of the baby-boomer era as we come of age together.

John Zielin and I climb a light post overlooking Fenway Park to watch the Boston Patriots play football. I am a four-letter man, coaching the Swaves in intramural baseball and football on the old Braves field, playing hockey and basketball. I study in the stacks of the Mugar Library with my cronies. I have a bit to drink and smoke and learn a few things about life.

Then in the summer of 1966 I am back home, working at a local restaurant in Worcester, Nick's Colonial Grill, as a busboy, which gave me spending money, but little else.

I am bowled over by Revolver, not quite sure what to make of the studio experiments of The Beatles, well aware they had created another masterpiece, yet so far removed from Rubber Soul.

The Beatles expressed dismay and disillusion in the album *Revolver*, released in early August of 1966. The album represents another marked change in their recording techniques: there is a decided influence of electronics and studio work, feats neither attempted nor experimented with in previous albums. The subject matter of the songs represents an enhanced attack on society. Less of the message is clothed in love songs. The Beatles began to branch into more far-reaching topics, yet retained a flavor of the simplicity and naiveté that brought their initial fame. *Revolver* represents a prime point in the evolution of The Beatles.

Chronologically, *Revolver* was released at the end of The Beatles' touring days. Ideologically the album represents a wider range of topics. *Revolver* is The Beatles' explosion at the evils of society. On the *Yesterday…and Today* album, The Beatles butchered man; on *Rubber Soul* they looked within, but on *Revolver* they took aim at social issues and fired their critiques in song.

The mood of *Revolver* embraces the wrongs and malpractice of society. From the breakdown of the family to cultural taboos on sex and morality, The Beatles exposed their private thoughts and feelings. The beginning of their critique against the "nowhere people" was launched in the summer of 1966, as The Beatles found they could take a stand on politics and social commentary in song. No wonder they felt *Revolver* was their most important album, the one that truly released them to be themselves.

Revolver encompasses subjects developed in later albums, but The Beatles initially set the tone here. *Revolver* was aimed at an anti-establishment audience. It provided the foundation for The Beatles experiments in Indian music and philosophy as well as the struggle for one's inner soul. They dabbled in drugs. *Revolver* became a radical extension of the love-song mantra. It was a biting criticism of the society The Beatles observed in 1966.

To ready their audience for the impending change in direction, from love songs to social commentary, The Beatles teased their fans with hints in their singles, early in 1966, shortly after the December

1965 release of *Rubber Soul*. These songs forecast the new direction for The Beatles.

"Dr. Robert" was a satire on the efficiency of the modern medical profession. Specifically the song was written about a New York physician who worked with the wealthy and prescribed pills for their every complaint. The Beatles found it humorous that a doctor kept NewYorkers high on pills. The song mocks the self-sacrifice of the good doctor. He'll address your every need with a pill. Supposedly, he makes you a better person, but in reality, he drugs his patients to mask their pain, which was more psychological than physical.

The implication was that with socialized medicine, the national health of England is both cheaper and more efficient. An ineffective physician survives, even thrives, in a corrupt system. Private doctors are more likely to make their patients wait longer and pay more for less; that is the subtext of the song. Yet the song concludes that Doctor Robert is not all bad. He is like a guru, a fool on the hill, who solves and salves the woes of his patrons. If you need him, he's there, day or night. And he's very good at what he does, even if it's feeding pills to an addled audience.

"Dr. Robert" satirized false promises physicians make. The implication was that doctors could cure human ills with special pills. The doctor The Beatles referred to allegedly was a Dr. Robert Freymann, who was very free with prescriptions of amphetamines. (Bono played the part of "Dr. Robert" in the movie that featured Beatle songs, *Across the Universe*, in 2007.)

Another angle of the song is that drug dealers were known as doctors. During the height of their touring days, The Beatles depended on their own "doctors," so they could down pills to make it through their next performance. That's what makes this a biting social commentary: The Beatles saw themselves as dependent on the drug dealer. It wasn't just Dr. Robert.

Around the time The Beatles recorded "Dr. Robert," in the first months of 1966, the Rolling Stones sang about "Mother's Little Helper," and offered another perspective on the same sorry saga. Adults are too strung out to spend time with their spouse or children; they go to the cabinet and pop a pill to calm down. They rely on instant cake or a frozen steak, instead of wholesome cooking. Valium can help you make it through the day, the Stones implied.

"Paperback Writer" is another satire, this time about writing cheap, probably raunchy, pulp fiction. The song is framed as a letter to a prospective publisher, a plea for recognition by a writer, rebuffed in his previous attempts at journalism. This morose drama, sung in an upbeat manner, reveals the plight of a fellow so desperate he can think of nothing better to do. Or the story reveals an author who tries to unload poor writing on an unsuspecting patron. In either case, it is a desolate lament.

The song switches from third to first person, and we are introduced to one of Lennon's more admired authors, Lewis Carroll. We wonder how much of this song is a play on Lennon's *A Spaniard in the Works,* his second collection of nonsense essays. Lennon was, indeed, a paperback writer.

Satire was the name of the game for The Beatles in mid-1966. They had made it in the pop music world, and now message rock was in vogue. They latched onto this new format with a tenacity and dexterity that again revealed their chameleon talents to mimic other musicians and perfect their style.

To express their own anathema at the social and political system which seemed alien to its citizenry, The Beatles launched a campaign in song directed against the nowhere people who dash through life with an emptiness in their soul. All the sane people can do is stand back and 'see how they run.' Like the white rabbit in *Alice in Wonderland,* these nowhere people are in such a hurry to get somewhere, they don't even know where they're going.

"And Your Bird Can Sing" was a slap at Mick Jagger and the Rolling Stones for their support of Marianne Faithfull. She was a budding singer, but Lennon felt she lacked the capacity of a star, hence the put-down. Jagger was wasting his time with her. The random lyrics give the song a throwaway feel, and Lennon considered it one of his worst tunes. The working title was "You Don't Get Me," and perhaps that sums up the qualities of the song.

"And Your Bird Can Sing" recounts the mockery of a woman who puts material possessions ahead of love, and in so doing, loses the essence of life. The choice is between money and love, and this girl isn't worth it. You may have all the material goods you want, but you can't buy me, you can't buy love. But when you grow weary of your worldly possessions, then I'll be ready for you. In other words, don't be dragged down by items of monetary worth; put your time and effort and love into personal relationships. That's where one finds real wealth.

"I'm Only Sleeping" attacked the nowhere people who run around. Other Beatle songs have lines which reference a similar attitude toward people unaware or unwilling to take advantage of the joys of life, people who lower themselves to menial or worthless tasks or find pleasure in material rather than spiritual rewards. The Beatles reminded their audience to wake up and live their lives more fully, rather than sit by and let things happen.

"See How They Run," may have been lifted from the old nursery rhyme "Three Blind Mice." Like mice, the nowhere people hurry aimlessly through life, never searching for anything of value, full of complaints and criticism about the world around them, following one another like sheep, blind to the beauty and potential of life. The Beatles attacked the man in the gray flannel suit, so intent on his own success and performance that he failed to see the rest of his family or the world around him.

In "I'm Only Sleeping," The Beatles look out at the nowhere

people in their world. They wrote about people who bother others for no reason. Yet this song is more than a critique on the aimlessness of man; it is a philosophical discussion on time and life, heavy subjects to discuss in song. The song opens with a Beatle waking up and looking around, believing he's still asleep and dreaming. He glances out the window at the nowhere people running around. He wants to be left alone, so he can go back to sleep. This is akin to watching an ant colony or a beehive in action, with each creature dashing around. For what?

The song delves into a deeper mode of attack on people "I'm Only Sleeping" is not just a simple pop poem about staying in bed. It is a satire on the pop star hero-worship which The Beatles, primarily John Lennon, sought to put behind them. The Beatles argue that their lives are not their own. They would rather not be bothered by the outside world; they resent interference. They want to be themselves, left alone to do their own thing. And isn't that just what their audience sought to hear? The Beatles advocated self-reliance and independence and used the metaphor of sleep to express a desire to escape. In this simple song they express a worldly philosophy of watching what's happening around them. The Beatles knew what was going on; they were awake, very aware, and they spoke their mind in song.

The Beatles made it clear they were fed up with pop-idol worship, tired of the adulation, weary of the tours. They want to be left alone, to watch the world go by, and take charge of their own lives. They had had enough of the fans and the press who prevailed in *A Hard Day's Night*, and now they hurried through life at such a speed they missed the beauty of solitude, the peace of being by oneself. It is no wonder The Beatles gave up touring that summer, retired from the hurly-burly of open-air concerts where screaming fans drowned out their words. They had served their public; now it was time to retire and write and record more significant work.

Watching the world slip by is a clear message that The Beatles had matters they wanted to work on, and when the time was right, would release them to the public.

They sought to use their time wisely. George Harrison quantified the import of the moment in the ballad "Love to You." Many of his phrases are clichés, but in their repetition they gain new meaning and more weighty significance.

Harrison sang about how fast time passes and how short our lives really are. You have to do as much as you can, and appreciate the opportunities that arise. Don't wait for someone else to do it for you. Harrison captured the passing moment and made it timeless. We know life is short, but is that an excuse to get things done or to let life slip through our fingers? He wanted to take advantage of whatever is possible. Like Lennon in "Nowhere Man," Harrison addressed the nowhere souls, who try to get something from you, and put their agenda on your back. This is a song about standing up for yourself, an extension of Harrison's "Think for Yourself."

Harrison's argument was to take advantage of the life we have, make the best and the most of it. He reached this conclusion from his study of Indian philosophy that we're all one, and each of us has the responsibility to be the best person we can be. Once more The Beatles predicted change and captured a mood among young people.

The Beatles' audience had matured with an awareness of social consciousness and responsibility. Grief over Kennedy's assassination had been assuaged by enthusiasm over The Beatles themselves. Now their audience was concerned about Vietnam, which had flamed into a full-blown military conflict. Lyndon Johnson was exerting his power through the military draft. An increasing number of young Americans had to face the possibility to going off to war. Fear and foreboding filled the air.

It wasn't just a foreign war that disturbed young people in 1966.

The civil-rights struggle exposed the plight of the black man with a war on the streets in the States. No longer could such events as a shooting or lynching or the beatings and arrests of Selma be relegated to the back pages. People coming of age in the mid-1960s looked out on a world of conflict: wealth and security for the richest people in the country and an army fighting a war overseas staffed by poor and black soldiers. Increased awareness of the inhumanity of man toward one another was a fact of life. The Beatles were no less aware than anyone else.

The Beatles assessed the political and social atmosphere of the world in 1966, and it had an effect on their decision to play a more active role in commenting on society. There was no future in touring, in singing "Please Please Me" in their late twenties. They recognized a growing awareness of the strata of society, the class structure, racism, and attitude toward the young. Consequently, Beatle songs began to reflect this divide. *Revolver* was a capable condemnation of the social and political system which the young generation viewed with increasing contempt.

The Beatles declared the basic fiber of society, its middle-class, was in a state of psychological decay. People who do not know or care why they live, destroy the lives of those who do care. The nowhere people become a burden on society because they are snobbish, haughty, wealthy, and powerful, and completely unaware of their own selves and the needs of those around them. People so intent on accomplishing certain goals or instituting certain restrictions on others, that they are unable to cope with chance and choice when it is presented to them, drag down those who care.

Ironically, in the midst of their own attack on society, The Beatles faced an attack on themselves.

The Beatles credence of love in 1965 on *Rubber Soul* backfired in the summer of 1966. An anti-Beatle crusade caught John Lennon off guard and taught The Beatles the disadvantage of forthright honesty.

A friendly London newspaper reporter asked Lennon his views on religion. His off-hand response was abbreviated to say The Beatles were more popular than Jesus Christ. The actual statement, which appeared in the London press on March 4, 1966, read: *"Christianity will go. It will vanish and shrink. I needn't argue about that: I'm right, and I will be proved right. We're more popular than Jesus Christ now; I don't know which will go first—rock and roll or Christianity. Jesus was all right, but his disciples were thick and ordinary. It's their twisting it that ruins it for me."*

Lennon derided a society that paid more adulation to rock idols than faith in religious leaders. His words were misinterpreted.

Months afterward, when the American press eventually uncovered this remark, the fervor it caused was overwhelming. Across the American South Beatle records were banned and burned by conservative Christian evangelicals. The Beatles were condemned by radio disc jockeys, fed by religious zealots who took offense at Lennon's remarks. It was ironic that the radio station that first organized a boycott of Beatle records had its transmitter blown off the air by a thunderbolt. As *Time* magazine summarized the tempest, "Reports of the death of Christianity, as Beatle John Lennon discovered this month, are greatly exaggerated."

Lennon was an astute and thoughtful observer of the culture that created The Beatles, but he misjudged the reaction to his comments. He was, however, a well-read social critic who investigated the roots of religion and the society that minimizes the value of God, yet magnifies the fame of its rock stars. Lennon found hypocrisy in both music and society: music should be a source of entertainment, not a sect or a cult. It is irrational for society to worship pop music stars as idols.

The trials The Beatles underwent during the summer of 1966 led to their final public performances. The Bible belt reaction to Lennon's statement gave The Beatles the justification they needed to retire from the concert circuit and return to the recording studio for the balance of their career. The stress of unwieldy concert arenas was no longer manageable. The Beatles' final live performance came at the end of their third American tour, at Candlestick Park in San Francisco, on August 29, 1966, shortly after the release of *Revolver*, their first studio album.

With touring behind them, The Beatles returned to Abbey Road, their recording studio sanctuary. This was the atmosphere The Beatles sought to compose and record in. Lennon and McCartney perfected their talents in peace, without the pressures of public performances. They put their touring suitcases away, not to be taken out until after their days as Beatles.

* * *

Revolver represented a new phase for The Beatles. They opposed the stuffed shirt, one-dimensional man. They gloried in the hope and expectations of people who care, who question society's goals, and help themselves and their fellow man. They admire people who know life and appreciate it.

The Beatles aimed *Revolver* at an audience concerned about the breakdown of the family structure as well as that of society. Their self-righteous anger is prevalent throughout the album and reflects the feelings The Beatles harbored through 1966.

The Beatles retained their patented love song, however, within the confines of its new theme. They subtly began an attack on social attitudes they disapproved of. The frame of reference, the direction of Beatles' music, was affected by this new focus, new awareness, and new power.

The song, "Rain" is simple, but there is a wealth of worry among the people running around to avoid a few drops of water. The nowhere people freeze in the face of change. They avoid the world around them, hiding from both rain and sun, unable, unwilling to appreciate the opportunities of darkness or light, water or air.

There is little more to this song, but the message of nowhere people, running away, avoiding reality, is evident. The Beatles mocked people afraid to take a chance, unwilling to accept the natural order of life. "Rain" never made it to number one, but did offer a unique twist to the music industry. Lennon played the end of the song in reverse, which created an otherworldly sound.

From the vague and nonspecific "Rain," The Beatles struck directly at the government in "Taxman," which debuted prominently on *Revolver*. Harrison, the bitter Beatle, wrote "Taxman" when he realized he was paying as much as 98% of his earnings in taxes. Thus this opening salvo of *Revolver* set the tone for the album. The Beatles were biting in their blatant attack, with not-so-subtle remarks against Prime Minister Edward Heath and Harold Wilson, leader of the Conservative Party in Parliament.

The taxman leaves you with a penny after he takes nineteen. Taxation is unreasonable and hits the wealthy the hardest. George is sarcastic in his plea to the government: they tax roads; soon they'll tax our feet. Next they will tax the heat. And then, in so many words, George implies that the workingman is laboring just to support the government. How fair is that? Never before had a music group delivered such a blistering attack on the revenue service. The little fellow got a big boost from this Beatles song.

Has any angry taxpayer ever written a more scathing attack? The Beatles were obviously outraged at the large chunk of their earnings that went to the government. The exorbitant tax on the wealthy drove many pop singers, like the Who, the Stones and The Beatles, to spend much of their time outside Great Britain.

(Ironically, H & R Block used "Taxman" in an advertisement early in 2002, months after George Harrison passed away.)

And so it was that The Beatles went from dabblers to dominators in message rock. As they moved, other rock groups followed The Beatles' led and began to criticize the world around them. Young people stood up for civil rights and against the draft. The generation gap widened with the expanded awareness of the world picture through the television screen and the words of songs in the music industry.

The nuclear family replaced the extended family, leaving the elderly to shift for themselves or in nursing homes. Children rebelled against the old school of discipline. Dr. Spock encouraged a more permissive view of child rearing. Instead of a son asking to borrow the car on a Saturday night, he expected it. The aggressiveness of teens was boosted by movies that promoted a more self-centered outlook. Teenagers were no longer isolated from politics, war, and civil strife; now these events were played out before their eyes on television. It was time for young people to assume a greater stake in their own lives.

The gap between generations was most evident in the family structure. As young people matured they started to seek their own identity. They put more weight on the words of their peers than their parents. This created the gap or split between generations. The younger generation grew restive, more rebellious, and gained strength simply in numbers. Increased awareness of social ills and impatience with a stodgy establishment created a more radical, volatile force among young people, making them willing to take matters in hand.

The Beatles were aware of these forces at work. They were naturally rebellious themselves; that was part of their mien. Being just a tad older than their audience, they anticipated which direction their fans were headed, and many times, The Beatles set the tone through their music. They were aware of societal changes happening around them, through contacts in the music and art worlds, and their own keen perceptions. With their extensive influence they wielded a power that must have felt limitless. The Beatles evolved into natural spokesmen for a generation ready and waiting for a revolutionary change in their lives.

Part of the charisma of The Beatles was a natural influence that came with their age, slightly older than the baby-boomers who were born after World War II. All four Beatles were born during the war, when Britain was under attack by the Nazis. It was posited by John Savage that The Beatles transferred a subconscious anger during the war into their loud, raucous rock music in the 1960s. Could such anger be harbored from birth?

Two of the most influential songs The Beatles wrote, in an effort to wake up the established older generation and energize the younger set, were the nowhere songs of 1966, which expressed dismay and disillusion with society. The songs were a pair of tunes, one generic, and the other specific. The frustration and anguish of the lonely people, the nowhere people, is evident in both songs.

The mournful tune, "Eleanor Rigby," describes a desolate life, full of despair.

Eleanor Rigby was one of the nowhere people who went through life with no one who really cared for her, or about her. Where do these people fit into society? She was religious, attending church, or at least, sadly, sweeping up the rice after a wedding. It was not her wedding. She had no children, and when she died, only the preacher was there for her. Or was he? Even the words of his sermon were not heard. This funeral was not for her. This life was not for her.

Paul originally named Daisy Hawkins as the protagonist, then appropriated the name Eleanor Rigby. One rumor was that it was the name of a ship moored along the pier in Liverpool. Another tale is that it is the name is on a gravestone in Liverpool's Woolton cemetery. This plot has become a stop on fan trips in Liverpool. Father McKenzie originally was Father McCartney until Paul paged through the phone book for someone other than his father. Ringo contributed the line about the pastor darning his socks. Elements of depression emanate throughout the song.

This is a telling lament of the abject misery of so many beautiful people who have so little to live for because their lives are so empty.

Who cared whether Eleanor lived or died? No one needed her. The loneliness of death was almost the answer to a prayer from the forgotten people of the world.

"Eleanor Rigby" stands as one of the more poignant songs The Beatles wrote. It is their signature effort to expose the loneliness of their fellow man. In its ability to describe the loneliness of so many people, the forgotten people of the world, it is without par.

"Eleanor Rigby" remains a remarkable tribute by The Beatles to the lost and lonely souls. The bitterness of life is evident, the inability to get to know Eleanor Rigby is clear. And the clergy, supposed to inspire hope in the destitute, fails dismally.

"Eleanor Rigby" was a product of a society that made thousands of lost and lonely people into outcasts, neglected because of race, age, or poverty. The song, "Eleanor Rigby," is ripe with the degradation and despair of a society that denies a happy life to its poor and forgotten people. This song has been considered a discourse on the death of the church. Reading the lines of the song is enough to feel the emptiness of the life of one parishioner.

McCartney was accused of plagiarizing Ezra Pound when Eleanor Rigby donned make-up that she kept by the door in a jar. The Beatles admittedly borrowed from influences all around them; that is why so much of their music feels so familiar.

The Beatles were blunt in their condemnation of the people in power who allow the emptiness in society to exist. They made it clear in "Taxman" that they opposed financial restraints on the citizenry. In "Eleanor Rigby" they decried the person who becomes a social outcast, the forgotten soul, with nothing to live for. The Beatles urged their audience to become more aware of personal goals, to take advantage of personal potential, to develop a point of view and express it. In the optimism of youth, they sought to live a life worth living. The Beatles urged their fans not to fall for a socio-political system that denies individual initiative. In short, The Beatles urged their audience to wake up and live for the moment.

"Eleanor Rigby's" counterpart was the amorphous "Nowhere Man." From the specific to the generic, The Beatles condemned the lost and lonely people, needlessly dashing through life. When John Lennon wrote "Nowhere Man," as one of the final songs on the British version of "Rubber Soul," he considered it autobiographic, just as he had cried out for Help! the year before. "Nowhere Man" was Lennon's attack on the weaknesses that lay within himself and within each of us.

But this song is also directed at nowhere people in general, not just Lennon. He makes plans which nobody follows. He is blind to opinions in the world around him. He has no motivation in life. All he has is own weak-linked perspective. In many ways, he is Eleanor Rigby, with nothing to live for, isolated and cast off by society.

This curt statement sums up the lives of many people, unable to appreciate the world for what it is. Like Sinclair in Hermann Hesse's young Demian, they have not yet realized the potential to be someone on their own. To blame the world through hate is to dislike part of oneself. Nowhere man has the potential to be someone but blames the world for his problems. Nowhere people are attached to their own miseries and complaints; they cannot see what is happening around them. They are, indeed, nowhere people, unable, unwilling, unready to face the potentials in their life.

"Eleanor Rigby" and "Nowhere Man" personify the ills of society, a society so caught up in itself it ignores the lonely and misguided. It is so rigid it fosters leaders unable to permit or encourage change in existing mores. The blunt beauty of these two songs is that they were written with a conscious concern so as not to offend their audience. It is clear what The Beatles were saying, but the songs themselves flow with such charming melody, the message blends seamlessly into a peaceful perspective of the world.

The Beatles managed to convey a variation on their message with the songs on *Revolver*. They still sang their own songs, but wove a cryptic or satiric message into the lyrics. They overwhelmed their audience with message rock. Though Bob Dylan set the pace in 1965, it was The Beatles who brought message rock to the fore in 1966 through the power of *Revolver*.

* * *

Another aspect of *Revolver* was the deeper, more intense love song. On the album, several songs point to disillusion and dismay, much more profound than the melancholy ballads of *Rubber Soul*. Two songs especially stand out as sad and lonely as they speak to a love that should have been, a love that could have lasted forever. But didn't.

Paul McCartney wrote "For No One." It is a simple song of a lover whose sweetheart has deserted him. Listening to the lyrics is a powerful experience; one can feel the anguish and dismay in the break-up of a love affair. The listener empathizes with the agony the bereft lover feels, as he longs for his partner. Everything he sees reminds him of her. Yet she is blind to his affection and has already moved on. Their love should have lasted, but didn't, and he acutely feels the sense of loss.

This potent poem describes feelings of rejection a spouse might experience whose mate has left: miserable, lonely, and lost. Because the partner is no longer there, the song could refer to a death, which, of course, is an irrevocable loss. Even the last note of the song is symbolically absent, and leaves the listener longing.

McCartney wrote this song in Switzerland as he recovered from a broken love affair. The working title was "Why Did It Die?" Paul and Ringo recorded it; George and John were not around for it in May 1966. McCartney hired a classical French horn player, Alan Civil, to add depth to the song. Mr. Civil thought he was to play a symphonic piece, "For No. One." Not quite! This song easily fits the genre of *Revolver*.

"Good Day Sunshine" described the confidence love can be, the flip side of "For No One." Now McCartney turned on the optimism only he could evoke. Here the lover basks in the sunshine of love, the glory of togetherness, the hope for a lengthy love affair. This is a happy, self-assured song, simple, but sincere. McCartney wrote this tune while lounging by Lennon's pool on a sunny afternoon, trying to emulate the Lovin' Spoonful in "Do You Believe in Magic," with their upbeat lyrics and hopeful manner. It's a casual, carefree song.

Another McCartney imitation is the beautiful "Here, There, and Everywhere," fashioned in the style of the Beach Boys' "God Only Knows." This is one of McCartney's favorite love songs, especially the way the lyrics mesh with the music and both flow seamlessly together. Love is a two-way street, as the persona describes. Both sides appreciate the affections expressed by the other. Love is very personal and affects a person deeply. To have a lover by your side makes everything seem better. Every little smile or wave of the hand is treasured. The song evokes a sense of assurance.

A profound sense of love makes a man feel he can face the world, knowing in his heart he has found true love. The hope that love never dies, that the couple remains together forever, protects the love affair through petty disagreements.

From McCartney's bubbling optimism, George Harrison described his love much more subtly. "I Want to Tell You" details the awkward nervousness of trying to express oneself. Harrison's tentative apologia sounds so sincere. The persona could say, "I don't mean to hurt you, but I get mixed up when I try to talk with you. I have so much I want to share, but I'm so nervous whenever I talk with you." An awkward teenager, just setting forth on his first romantic endeavor, would likely sound this way.

Harrison's search for security was evident in his plea. He was aware of his inadequacies, but unable to overcome them. This was a new relationship he wanted to succeed, but recognized he had difficulty expressing himself. He lacked the courage to talk to this girl, and needed to gain self-confidence to handle the situation. There is an earnest sincerity in his struggle. A couple of working titles for this song were "I Don't Know" and "Laxton's Superb." (Years later Harrison revised a line of the song to read, "It isn't me, it's just the mind," which removed responsibility for his inability to express himself.)

Even as George Harrison wrote about his inadequacies in expressing himself, he was becoming more respected as a lyricist with The Beatles. *Revolver* is the first album in which Harrison had three songs; in the previous albums, he was allowed only two.

Beatle fans identified with George Harrison's honesty and looked to his words when they found themselves in situations in which they had no control. Doubting their own abilities, they wondered which choice to make. Harrison capitalized on that instinctive indecision, such a big part of adolescence. His penetrating personal contributions added a unique dimension to the appeal of The Beatles. And his honest approach to love met the needs of a legion of fans.

* * *

The Beatles still sang love songs, even as they attacked society, though they often cloaked their antagonistic comments in words of love. It can be a challenge to discern whether they spoke as lonely lovers or critical idealists; that points to the universality of their lyrics. The metaphor of a love affair was closely encoded in each song, so it became the symbol, as well as the system, for their communication.

"What Goes On" was the only song credited to three of The Beatles: John, Paul and Ringo. John initially wrote it in his Quarryman days, and The Beatles wanted to record and release it in 1963, as a reprise to "Please Please Me," but it didn't make the cut. With a little re-writing, "What Goes On" was squeezed onto the British version of *Rubber Soul*, and only arrived in the States on *Yesterday...and Today*, with the leftover hits, repackaged and released in the States on June 14, 1966.

The song is simple, about a girl the persona met earlier that day. She enchanted him. Now, time has passed, and feelings have changed. The persona realized he missed what she was thinking about, and is unhappy at the way she treats him.

The Beatles mixed the metaphor of a love affair with the depth of feeling that, as they were getting older, life was passing them by. They still had an emotion to express and had to work to extract and expand on it as much as possible.

Arrogance and disdain, pride and piety, glamour and show are expected of the movie star or popular singer. When The Beatles translated this arrogance to their music through a love song, they accomplished an exacting feat: simultaneously they spoofed themselves and made fun of their contemporaries and critics.

Harrison's "If I Needed Someone" is pompous and proud, reminiscent of a lover who has all the girls he can handle. He is arrogant, as only a pop idol can be, who has no use for the critics or respect for his fans. The Beatles stated they did not seek any more fame or adulation; they had made it and wanted to be left alone to do their own thing. (This song could be considered a sequel to Harrison's earlier tune, "Don't Bother Me.") The idea that the persona is self-sufficient negates the need for human contact. Harrison's sense of isolation was more intense than his fellow Beatles.

When George Harrison wrote "If I Needed Someone," it was an effort to mimic the Byrds in "The Bells of Rhymney." This was the only Harrison song The Beatles sang on their last tour across the States in the summer of 1966.

George Harrison recognized that The Beatles had made it and no longer needed the support of the press. But the line about saving a place for your number brought a bit of humor to the situation. They may still need someone, so don't wander too far.

The lonely lover was transformed to social critic. Harrison reacted to an audience now adept at recognizing the social injustices of the world. The critic sought solutions to the problems caused by society with its misplaced sense of values. The Beatles both promulgated the sense of doubt, and reacted to the errant society which stumbled along. In a larger sense, they prompted their fans to get involved.

* * *

In 1966, The Beatles entered a surrealistic phase as they produced several haunting tunes, quite different from previous efforts. The pervading mood of these songs was one of despair and disillusion. The Beatles tuned out their optimistic attitudes and concentrated on futile struggles. Two songs from *Revolver* set the tone of dismay, which pointed a new direction for The Beatles.

The Beatles were holed up in Beverly Hills in the late summer of 1965. They visited with the likes of Joan Baez and spent time with Elvis Presley. And they took acid.

"She Said She Said" is a morose dialogue between Peter Fonda and John Lennon. The images Fonda conjured up were the basis for this song, which has a decidedly otherworldly feel. It is a question and answer format, presented in a dreamy manner, as the words and sounds creep out at the listener.

This strange, mystical tune was a means for The Beatles to conjure up an otherworldly exploration of death. The sense of not being alive, but still experiencing what is going on, is a unique take on Eastern philosophical thought. There is sadness and sorrow in this song. At the same time they explored the dismay they found in a stagnant society.

"She Said She Said" contains one of the premier percussion performances by Ringo Starr. His drumming brought the song to life, and was an apt inclusion to the *Revolver* recording sessions.

The first song The Beatles recorded for *Revolver* ironically was the last song on the album: "Tomorrow Never Knows." This most melancholy dirge is one of John Lennon's more profound statements. The song says a lot and means a lot: it is both an escape from, and attempt to deal with, reality. It is religious and heretical at once, a veritable clash of ideas, just what Lennon loved to sink his mind into. Universal love is equivalent to the oneness of life. The internal workings of the mind are reflected in the excitement of society. The mysticism of this song makes it well worth reading.

Unwind and let yourself drift off. Give in and give up, and you'll find the essence of life within. The song advocates meditation, in this sense, but also promotes the age-old adage that love is all around us; we just have to let ourselves go to feel it. Love is all knowing, all believing, all caring. It is what life is all about.

"Tomorrow Never Knows" expresses unity and cohesion, yet in

a mournful manner. Funereal in its production, "Tomorrow Never Knows" sets out a sense of completion, of harmony, of satisfaction, that all is done as it should be; yet the misery and sorrow linger.

Lennon was inspired to write "Tomorrow Never Knows" after reading *The Psychedelic Experience* by Timothy Leary, Richard Alpert, and Ralph Metzner, which interpreted the Tibetan *Book of the Dead*. Lennon wanted the song to sound like the Dali Lama, and sought Tibetan monks to chant in the background. Instead, tape loops and vocal double tracking was employed, a much more efficient source of sound. The initial name of the song was "Mark 1;" another title was "The Void," but Ringo coined the phrase, "Tomorrow Never Knows," an appropriate appellation for this philosophical diatribe.

Like so many songs, this was unique in the annals of Beatle discography. It was a joint collaboration between Lennon and McCartney, inspired by an outside influence. It was a cryptic, mournful tune that explored the hopelessness of life. It expressed The Beatles' feelings and fears of death, yet showed their skill at translating thoughts and emotions to song. The essence is that The Beatles urged their audience to accept themselves and prevent hatred and misery from ruining their lives. The need for compassion toward our fellow man is evident.

And so *Revolver* marks a close. There are hints of a new direction for The Beatles, but nothing specific.

Revolver represented The Beatles' first studio album, a collection of songs which could not be reproduced on stage. The Beatles considered *Revolver* the most enjoyable album they produced. This was, in part, because they found freedom in the recording studio. (In 2002 the readers of Rolling Stone magazine named *Revolver* the best album of all time.)

Revolver proved a pinnacle in its creativity. The Beatles put their all into *Revolver*, yet it turned out to be a trial run for the real thing. Its cover speaks to the depth of The Beatles, as well as their search for simplicity. Klaus Voormann, a buddy from their days in Hamburg, sketched the cover, giving it a casual, modern touch.

As they began to raise the consciousness of their audience, they simultaneously raised the bar for themselves. As they stored their touring suitcases and headed back into the recording studio in the fall of 1966, they prepared to embark on a most ambitious effort. *Revolver* was a necessary precursor to the masterpiece The Beatles created over the subsequent six months.

Their magnum opus would be created and released within a year of *Revolver*.

* * *

John Zielin (techie/teacher/Buddhist): *"Beatles…hmmm. My introduction? 'I Want to Hold Your Hand' comes first to mind… a pop song that thrilled me in my teens…. along with so many other pop songs in that early Beatles phase…. then the slow evolution of The Beatles and myself…. 'All You Need Is Love' comes to mind… my confused 'What's it all about?' phase…finding meaning and figuring out who I was (that has never ended)…. 'Living is easy with your eyes closed. It's understanding all you see.' It getting hard to be someone… the political understanding…. the war in Viet Nam apparently we have not progressed very far in 'freeing your mind instead'…. hmmm …. as I write this, I realize how woven into my being The Beatles are…their evolution paralleled my evolution…. their words languaged my confusing growth…they are such a gift to a searching tumbling planet…. "pools of sorrow and waves of joy"….. "limitless and undying love"…call me "all along across the universe"…. "into the light of the dark black night." Those are my kaleidoscopy reflections of The Beatles."*

Kevin Begley (carpenter): *"So much time since we were in Pepperland. The pressure and boredom of touring was now being put behind them, no more 'trained fleas' performing for the masses, as John put it.*

Beatlemania was a drag. After the last concert in San Francisco, George declared, 'That's it. I'm not a Beatle anymore.' That was at the end of August 1966.

"The next summer would be the 'summer of love.' Despite all the dissolution and dissonance among the 'Fabs,' much more fantastic music was to be created. Their incredible output of singles, albums and touring over the past few years was at an end. The respite would prove to be well worth the wait and take us all in unimagined directions.

"John's poignant nostalgic look back to his bygone youth first surfaced with 'In My Life' and was now to be explored again with 'Strawberry Fields Forever', this wistful poem to childhood haunts inspiring Paul's response with 'Penny Lane.' Both songs recorded and released prior to **Pepper** *almost found their way onto the album. Prior contractual agreements required them to be released as a & b sides of a single.*

"As a testament to their work ethic and genius, coupled with behind-the-scenes breakdowns on multiple levels, they came out with **Sgt. Pepper**, *released June 1, 1967, in America. Mostly Paul's concept, yet interesting and new contributions from everyone. A major turning point in recording methods, subjects, and new sounds. One of the first albums to have the lyrics printed on the record cover. Seems so commonplace today, yet another innovation which just put the cherry on top.*

"Largely unknown to us and perhaps to The Beatles themselves at the time was that this was the beginning of the end. They were growing up and apart from one another. There were more great albums to come, yet changes were taking place. George's Indian influences, emerging spiritual quest and disaffection with Paul's enthusiasm for control were driving them apart. John's disintegrating marriage to his ever-faithful college sweetheart Cynthia, his own flagging confidence… 'I'm a Loser,' 'Nowhere Man,' along with his heavy use of LSD, was taking its toll. Ringo remained the steadfast keeper of the backbeat and beautifully syncopated pudding tom-tom drum fill. His developing style always in sync with the nature and feel of a tune, no matter its chord, sequence or time changes.

"There is also the tragic winding down of Brian Epstein's usefulness to the group and his own dissolution over his personal life, his intake of pills and crumby business decisions all weighing him down. His early death comes at the end of August 1967. The troubled soul who saw the potential in those cheeky, leather-clad rock and rollers playing their hearts out in the dank, damp, darkness of a cellar club called the Cavern. To John's credit, he put Stuart Sutcliffe's picture on the **Pepper** cover, his close friend from college days. With them in the beginning, but not destined for musical stardom, Stuart's life ending sadly somewhere in Hamburg from a brain hemorrhage.

"And so with a shelter in the middle of a roundabout to visit, along with many other places, a mythology and history develop."

Chapter Eight:
Sgt. Pepper's Lonely Hearts Club Band— June 1, 1967

I travel through Europe in 1967, arriving in London on May 30. In storefront windows all over the city I see the gatefold jacket of **Sgt. Pepper**, *with The Beatles in full parade regalia. I am overwhelmed with their impressive production.*

Hitchhiking in the west of England, in Wales, I ride with a truck driver who jovially claims he once worked with Ringo Starr, back in Liverpool. Not sure what they did together, but he is pretty proud that he knew Ringo way back when.

In Liverpool I see a bus with the words, 'Penny Lane' on the destination board. And of course I find the street. I remember the cathedral, bombed by the Germans in World War II and rebuilt in a modern manner. It has little to do with The Beatles but memorializes the war, and the era they grew up in.

Eurailing through Europe I hear snippets of 'All You Need is Love' and listen to the entire song when I duck into an Amsterdam record store, withdraw into a little booth in back, don headphones, and drift off with those wondrously universal words. I'd read about the Our World concert, broadcast to some 70 million people. The Beatles wrote this song specifically for that event. When I hear the song, I know they had come through once more.

I never actually listen to **Sgt. Pepper** *in its entirety until I return to the*

IT WAS 40 YEARS AGO TODAY

States in September. I sat with my brothers, realizing The Beatles had reached their peak performance.

Sgt. Pepper's Lonely Hearts Club Band. The title itself raises a host of questions. Who was Sgt. Pepper? What is the Lonely Hearts Club? Was this for real, or had The Beatles lost their collective mind?

The Beatles released *Sgt. Pepper* in England on Thursday, June 1, 1967, and the next day in the United States. For the first time, both the American and British versions of a Beatle record were identical. It took 129 days to record the album—their magnum opus.

Sgt. Pepper became an event that inspired an entire counterculture. It expanded the boundaries of rock and roll and raised the bar for studio experimentation.

By late summer 1966, The Beatles had wearied of the pressures of touring. The concert venue was fraught with tension; screams drowned out their songs, and an element of fear crept into public appearances. And significantly, touring took them away from their creative element: the recording studio. That fall Paul suggested they retreat to the sanctity of the studio and create music as the members of an imaginary band. The fictitious band led to a concert, complete with an imitation audience, and *Pepper* was born.

If there is one album The Beatles are known for, it's *Sgt. Pepper*. The Beatles poured everything they had into *Pepper*, and it shows. It is a superb album in every facet and remains a unique expression of their talent, forty years after its release.

Sgt. Pepper was a conceptual concert from its opening song. The initial tune was reprised near the end, and accompanied by an imaginary audience clapping. Until *Pepper*, rock albums had been a collection of tunes with nothing to bind the songs together. Producer George Martin arranged each song to run into the next, which literally tied the album together.

Sgt. Pepper dealt with topical themes, relevant to young people of the late 1960s. It was released at the beginning of the summer of love, yet is laden with forebodings of loneliness and death. In many ways, the album represents rebellion in its quest for self-discovery. For the hippie movement in that long-ago summer, it became the musical bible.

The album influenced life styles around the world. From San Francisco to New York, from Rome to Paris, from Tokyo to Bombay, *Sgt. Pepper* made an impact. It condoned the use of drugs. It described the plight of the runaway. It honored rebellion. While it recognized friendship, it toyed with love. It respected old age, yet honored youth. *Pepper* was an album of self-actualization, and crystallized with fans who latched onto the words from their turntable in that long-ago early June of 1967. And much of *Pepper* still resonates today.

Pepper provided an imaginary stage for The Beatles to perform. It forced fans to accept The Beatles as gurus instead of pop idols.

In *Sgt. Pepper*, The Beatles satisfied their own cries for help. They took the conventional love song well beyond the nostalgia of *Rubber Soul* and honed down the avarice of *Revolver*. *Sgt. Pepper* fine-tuned themes which increasingly had become part of The Beatles' repertoire.

It had been six months since the release of *Revolver*, touring days were behind them, there was no movie on the horizon, and fans were curious what The Beatles were up to. Critics said they had dried up, with nothing new to offer. Not quite. To prepare their audience for the extraordinary album they were working on, The Beatles released two singles in February 1967 which anticipated their new direction.

"Strawberry Fields Forever" and "Penny Lane" was the first double-A Beatles single. Both songs took a wistful look back on The Beatles' youth, from very different perspectives.

"Strawberry Fields Forever," by John Lennon, was a dreamy self-analytic song. Strawberry Fields was a Salvation Army Children's Home, near the house where Lennon lived in Woolton, a Liverpool suburb. He enjoyed attending garden parties there in his youth. The orphanage grounds were public enough so a young man could bring a girl to get to know her, relax, and escape reality.

(In his post-Beatle years, Lennon donated money to Strawberry Fields, and Lennon Hall was named for him. In 2005, the orphanage was closed, and the remaining children assigned to a group home. The site is popular on tours of Liverpool.)

On another level "Strawberry Fields" is an individual's search for self, leading into a drug-induced trance, or a personal trek of self-discovery. The tone of isolation and an unreal sense of the world evoke the fantasy world discovered through drugs.

The Beatles first smoked marijuana when Bob Dylan met with them in the States in 1964. By 1965 John and George had taken acid trips and soon introduced LSD to Paul and Ringo. Two years later The Beatles knew their audience could grasp that a very potent experience awaited them. Slyly, they hinted that drugs could turn you on, a joint would open your mind, and acid would go that much further.

Looking back at his youth through wire-rimmed, rose-tinted, drug-enhanced lens, Lennon described being lost and the struggle to find himself. His song is filled with clichés woven seamlessly into his tale of self-discovery, and is ripe with psychedelic references and a surreal sense of reality. The original title was "It's Not Too Bad," which imbues the song with an optimistic flavor.

The song fades out, then comes back, echoing its earlier beat, a facet that frustrated DJs who didn't know how to handle the false ending. Lennon mutters, "Cranberry sauce," later construed as, "I buried Paul." An otherworldly pall drapes the message. The song elicits the best of Lennon's hypnotic wordplay. "Strawberry Fields

Forever" symbolized the dream world where everything works out but doesn't matter anyway. That's the magic and the mystery.

"Penny Lane," on the other hand, is a tribute to a downtown thoroughfare in Liverpool. Paul McCartney concocted his story around the merchants in the community. He sought to recall his roots in a simple story that may also be a drug trip. The whimsical plot revolves beneath the township's azure skies. A fireman rushes into a barbershop in the pouring rain, yet beneath the clear blue suburban sky, an image that draws the listener into the tale.

This is a (bus) trip down memory lane, peeking in the windows of the storekeepers. The song is upbeat, a wistful recollection of those carefree days of long ago. The basis for the song was that in their youth, John and Paul would meet at Penny Lane and take the bus downtown. Sitting at the shelter, Paul noted the barbershop, owned by a Mr. Bioletti, the fire station, Barclay's Bank, and of course the roundabout (rotary) where a pretty nurse once sold flowers.

(The roundabout is gone, replaced by a restaurant, appropriately titled Sgt. Pepper's Bistro. Also gone, over the years, are the street signs for Penny Lane. Tired of frequently having to replace them, the city took to painting the street name on nearby buildings.)

An amusing aspect to "Penny Lane" is that Paul, The Beatles' public-relations persona, inserted a little off-color humor with his line about a finger pie. Like the chorus of "Girl," repeating the word, "tit," The Beatles added humor and inside jokes wherever possible.

McCartney's reminiscence stands in stark contrast to Lennon's dream, but the songs complement one another admirably. They brim with the nostalgia kindled in *Rubber Soul* even as they foster the avant-guard experimentation of *Revolver*. Perhaps most importantly, the double-A single prepared the public for what lay ahead with *Sgt. Pepper*.

These two songs were intended to be included on the *Sgt. Pepper* album, and in many ways they epitomize the *Pepper* style. However, Capital Records decided to release them early, intent on recovering The Beatles' prominence after the debacle over Lennon's "anti-Christ" remark, the end of The Beatles' touring schedule, and the dearth of songs since the release of *Revolver*.

This was the first Beatle single in four years not to reach number one. Sales were calculated on both songs, as it was a double-A record. George Martin considered this the premier single The Beatles ever released, although he could have capitalized on the songs by releasing them as two separate singles.

Fans played this record repeatedly through the propitious spring of 1967. Something was happening, something big, but for the moment, the music world could only wait. The Beatles teased their audience. Anticipation was fueled by rumors that the new album would cost upwards of $100,000, yet be distributed in a plain brown wrapper.

When *Sgt. Pepper* was eventually released in a vibrant gatefold jacket, with the lyrics printed on the back, it proved much more than anyone anticipated. A photograph of the resplendent Beatles stood on the cover, clutching their instruments. Over a flowered grave of The Beatles, Madame Tussaud's wax images of the Fab Four looked on. Was this a symbolic death and an opportune rebirth? Dozens of favorite famous people stood behind them. Inside were imposing headshots of John, Paul, George, and Ringo, in psychedelic *Pepper* regalia, complete with decorator badges and epaulets. It was June 2, 1967, when *Sgt. Pepper* hit the States, and the world has not been the same since.

From the opening bars of *Sgt. Pepper* and the words of the Lonely Hearts Club Band, the theme of loneliness is developed. Over 37 minutes, through thirteen songs, a sense of desolation pervades and unites the album. The concept is carried to the end where we are left with a feeling of emptiness at all the potholes in the roads of Lancashire.

Loneliness is prevalent among the young and very old. That was key to the divide between generations. 1967 was the year of the hippie, a lonely character in search of self. From San Francisco to Central Park, young, bedraggled vagabonds symbolized a wish for love and peace and epitomized loneliness. Flower people populated poorer parts of urban areas. Hippies were filled with love and peace in theory, but their lives were often wracked with despair and rejection. They rebelled against authority from their parents, their school, the Army, the workforce, society. They sought a better life but weren't sure how to attain it.

The hippie movement latched onto *Sgt. Pepper* and nominated The Beatles as spokesmen for a philosophy of escapism from the loneliness of life. The Beatles offered a cloak of love and fantasy in the imaginary world of *Sgt. Pepper*. Young people perceived the album as a testament for the summer of love. And they listened to the songs over and over. One cannot exaggerate the impact *Sgt. Pepper* had on the youth movement.

While The Beatles had been aloof from issues of youth when they sang their spirited love songs, they now plunged into the midst of the generation gap. To bring this attitude to the fore, they looked within and emerged with songs that bespeak the struggles and dreams of disenchanted youth.

It may have been coincidence, or cause and effect, but in the short summer of 1967, The Beatles emerged as shamans of a generation of young people who sought to make the world a better place, a new direction for a society they felt had failed them.

The Beatles met the challenge of youth by becoming spokesmen through a raft of songs that fed the needs of the lost and lonely people. Nostalgic references accentuated the sense of loneliness. The theme of *Sgt. Pepper* was in harmony with the hippie movement, and the words and emotions mimicked the feelings of the communes and be-ins on the street.

Like prophets, The Beatles anticipated the summer as a time of free love and understanding for a better world. The unshaven, hungry, wanton hippies shared each other's hearts and souls, bodies and coins, food and shelter. Perhaps *Pepper* caused the hippie movement; more likely it spurred a sense of self-discovery already underway. The summer of 1967, from the communes in Haight-Ashbury, California, to the hoards of hippies from Oslo to Rome, blossomed as if emerging from a cocoon and flourished in that long lost summer of love. It was a magical time. And *Sgt. Pepper* assumed the role of the herald as he sounded the populace to bask in the bounty and beauty of the wondrous creation by The Beatles.

* * *

From the opening sounds of the audience settling down, *Sgt. Pepper* builds. The first side brims with songs of friendship, drugs, a smidgeon of nostalgia, a runaway, and a carnival. The second side digs down to the depths of despair and reaches upward toward the concept of self-examination and self-actualization.

The concept for *Sgt. Pepper* allegedly originated on an airplane flight when Beatle aide Mal Evans asked Paul what the little packets labeled S and P were on his meal tray. Paul used the initials to create the *Sgt. Pepper* image, which he imagined as a concept album. It was a major leap forward in music history.

We, as the imaginary audience, are admonished to calm down and listen as the band starts to play. The performers are introduced and we learn the singer's name is Billy Shears, which turns out to be Ringo Starr, and the intro segues into "With a Little Help from My Friends." McCartney and Lennon wrote this song especially for Ringo, and limited the range so he could handle it.

(Lennon originally called it "Bad Finger Boogie," as he'd hurt his forefinger. Later, the Apple band Badfinger got its name from this title. "With a Little Help from My Friends" inspired the British reality television show, where a celebrity performs an act of charity, with a little help from his friends.)

The song is set up as a response between the singer and the audience. It was written at Paul's house, with John and Paul playing around. Ringo made one revision to the original line which was "Would you stand up and throw tomatoes at me?" He feared a public response akin to the jelly beans fans tossed at The Beatles after George's off-hand remark that The Beatles liked jelly babies.

The audience applause between songs was recorded at the Hollywood Bowl Concert at the end of the summer of 1966.

Friends counteract loneliness. "With a Little Help from My Friends" is a ballad of give and take, question and answer, wants and needs. The Beatles admonish one who is sad to seek out friends to help get one by. Humanity needs interaction, and The Beatles praised it in song. They acknowledged the need to be part of a social network.

Maybe they couldn't save the world, but friends could make life more tolerable.

Love is the key ingredient to combat loneliness. The Beatles did not focus on individual love in *Sgt. Pepper*, rather they gave credence to love of mankind. The unity of the hippies, an agreement in principle as well as life style, was evidenced in song. The flower-power generation gained support from The Beatles. The affinity young people had for one another was a constant throughout the summer of 1967 and beyond.

The generation that emerged from the post-war baby-boom, survived the nuclear fears of the late 1950s, and mourned the death of Kennedy in 1963, now embraced one another with a group identity which crystallized in *Sgt. Pepper*.

The third song on the album took a very different tack. The initials of "Lucy in the Sky with Diamonds," the dream sequence, and the illusions bespeak a different origin. Much of Lennon's work was influenced by Lewis Carroll and *Alice in Wonderland*. John Lennon did not want to reference his use of drugs to recreate a furor, as he had with his views on religion, so he passed the onus to his son Julian, and humorously hid his not-so-subtle subject matter from prim-and-proper pundits.

Ostensibly "Lucy in the Sky with Diamonds" was written about a little girl in Julian's class at Heath House School. Her name was Lucy O'Donnell, and she lives in Surrey. Another Lucy, Lucy Richardson, may have inspired the song. And Peter Cook's daughter was Lucy, another option.

(In 1974 "Lucy in the Sky with Diamonds" was playing on the radio when paleoanthropologist Donald Johanson discovered a three million year old pre-human fossil in Africa. He named this oldest human ancestor Lucy, in honor of the song.)

Life was "Getting Better." There was hope. No need to dwell on the past, except to build for the future, The Beatles seemed to say. Anger harbored in school or toward parents could be focused in a constructive manner so we could work to help one another.

McCartney came up with the words to "Getting Better" while walking his sheepdog Martha on a bright sunny day. He composed the song, then Lennon added his take, bringing the words down to his reality. The innocent naiveté of McCartney was bluntly contrasted with the pessimism of Lennon, who looked back on his past behavior, recognized his faults, and admitted his failings. McCartney took those failings and felt that life was improving. The overall impression is that this is a song of hope, even in a world that struggled with challenging social issues.

The Beatles captured youthful bitterness toward an ephemeral establishment. In "Getting Better" they offered an option out.

McCartney's sense of optimism flourished in this song, and it is what many people took from *Pepper*. One gets a sense that with a little love and understanding, we can make it.

The positive outlook prevailed. A fresh attitude could overcome past mistakes. Beatle songs offer hope but hand responsibility to the individual to make it happen.

"Getting Better" is the most upbeat tune on the album, even with its somber undertone. It fits into the vein of "With a Little Help from My Friends," but makes pointed reference to self-appreciation, rather than a dependence on companionship.

Promoting self-improvement, Paul McCartney composed "Fixing a Hole," which compares the mind to a room, a room where the persona protects himself from the craziness in the world around him. The song has the feel of letting one's mind wander, whether on drugs, or the freedom of self-exploration.

The inspiration of the song has multiple facets, from patching a pothole in the road to repairing the barn roof at McCartney's Scottish sheep farm. "Fix" and "hole" allude to heroin, though The Beatles naturally denied that intent.

"Fixing a Hole" links the physical attributes of a room: floor, walls, door, windows and roof, with what is happening around us. We are rooms unto ourselves. It is up to each of us to make our room as habitable as possible. No one can turn our minds into something we don't want, and the silly people who argue, as they hurry aimlessly by, distract us from our purpose in life, from ourselves. "Fixing a Hole" was a way station to improve the self. "Fixing a Hole" spoke to the lost and lonely people who put *Sgt. Pepper* on their turntable and never stopped playing it during that summer of love.

"She's Leaving Home." Escape. Runaway from home. Find a new life. Leave the past behind. That was the message. The runaway became a challenge as the summer wore on. Congregating in cities with like-minded kids built a sense of camaraderie, but this did not bode well for the future. It was escapist rather than dealing with the reality of living at home.

A newspaper article inspired the song. On February 27th, 1967, the *London Daily Mirror* headline read: "A-level girl dumps car and vanishes." That girl was 17-year-old Melanie Coe. She returned home a week later. Ms. Coe actually met Paul McCartney three years after her adventure. She didn't run off with a car salesman, as the song implied, but rather a casino worker, a croupier.

Nineteen sixty-seven proved a coming-of-age era for many people, and *Pepper* was part of the inspiration. "She's Leaving Home" is filled with well-worn phrases that described the confusion of parents who buy their child everything. The child spurns her parents' efforts, and both experience a devastating loss, wondering what went wrong. The poignant words are laced with clichés, yet the simple song spoke directly to many people.

As the child leaves home, the parents feel unappreciated, and foist guilt on their progeny. The child cannot grasp the heartache her departure causes. The power of the words resonates. It is complete disconnect. The Beatles spoke to an audience who had experienced these events. John Lennon said he wrote the song for his Aunt Mimi, who brought him up when his mother died. He challenged her every step of the way. Lennon added the Greek chorus, with the parents' refrain about giving their child anything they thought she wanted.

"She's Leaving Home" was The Beatles' signature song on the runaway. As poignant as "Eleanor Rigby," but more personal, and with a young heroine rather than an older woman, the song reverberated up and down the East and West coasts that summer of love, played out in numerous similar situations. The telling tale is as poignant today as it was when it hit the streets, all those years ago.

The last song on the first side of the album, "Being for the

Benefit of Mr. Kite," exudes the carnival atmosphere Lennon avidly sought when the song was recorded. Appropriated from the words of a 19th century poster Lennon picked up in an antique shop, the lyrics describe acts featured at Pablo Fanque's Circus Royal. Background sounds include a fairground organ and calliope spliced in tape snippets to give an unusually festive feel to the tune. Mr. J. Henderson is listed as the celebrated somerset thrower, and trampoline leaps are featured.

"Being for the Benefit of Mr. Kite" could have been a throwaway, yet some consider it the most appropriate song on the album. It captures the gaiety of a performance designed to entertain. Beneath the surface, however, lurks a sadness for the circus performers, destined to repeat their act over and over, with a tired hope to entertain, guaranteed to amuse, sure to amaze. The show is listed as "The grandest night of the season." And "Being for the Benefit of Mr. Kite" reverberates to this day, ensuring satisfaction at every turn.

In 1967 it was time to turn the long-playing record album over and listen to side two. George Harrison's signature contribution to *Sgt. Pepper* was "Within You, Without You." Harrison claims the nowhere people hold us back, and life is found within oneself. All of us have the power to attain our goals. No one can do that for us. The individual reigns supreme, yet life goes on without us. No one is indispensable.

The Beatles reached a very personal level on *Sgt. Pepper*, when they explored the loneliness within. That's where the deeper meaning of *Pepper* is uncovered. The individual feels lonely in that he doesn't know who he is. That road to discovery is the essence of *Sgt. Pepper*. The search for identity was the underlying theme of this epic work.

The individual can realize his potential, but it requires work. It cannot be done for him. The concept is that we are all one, joined together in love. Love of our fellow man can save us from the loneliness that fills our lives. Harrison encouraged his audience to see that we are all one, but the individual must make it on his own.

Harrison critiqued the lost and lonely masses, and sang of the universality of love, the importance of self-awareness and felt that love is all around us, if we only open our hearts. The influence of Indian religion is evident in "Within You, Without You." Western homilies are interspersed with Eastern philosophies in this majestic melody. Harrison's masterpiece combines themes from both cultures. His audience treasured every word, believing he spoke with the authority of a mystic who can bring us to a higher level of understanding.

The song is laden with Hindu ideas, the Maya, that life is a false reality, the Dharma, that we must save the world from destruction, and Monism, that we are all one. Harrison advocated self-examination rather than waiting for a God or prophet to save us. The concept of water flowing is evident in eastern philosophies and that opens the theme of reincarnation. We've all been here before, and we'll be back! (Harrison believed in reincarnation, and when he died of cancer in 2001, his Eastern beliefs made death more bearable.)

The song was reduced from its initial 30 minutes to five minutes and five seconds for the album. The peals of laughter at the end were added to lift the mood from such a heavy topic and ease back into the *Pepper* mindset.

This ponderous piece offered a philosophical basis for the summer of love. The serious tone of a beautiful Indian raga, based on the efforts of Ravi Shankar, was supplemented by classical Indian musicians as back-up, with assistant Neil Aspinall playing the tambura. The depth of feeling behind the message of "Within You, Without You" is evident today. This was the last song recorded in the creation of *Sgt. Pepper*.

Paul McCartney was 24 when he recorded "When I'm Sixty-Four." McCartney originally played the melody as a teenager with Lennon and the Quarrymen in the late 1950s, but added the lyrics in 1967 for his widowed father who had just turned 64.

The song has the sound of a hurdy-gurdy piano piece. Producer George Martin fashioned it after the 1920s big-band sound, and it came to be known as retro-rock. In the final verse, a clarinet harmonizes neatly with McCartney's voice, a unique accomplishment in 1966. Martin was going to put this song on a single with "Penny Lane." That he didn't, he considers one of the biggest mistakes of his career.

"When I'm Sixty-Four" is a wistful sharing of dreams, after meeting someone later in life. This song is appropriately about a lonely hearts club, though it dwells more on the past. On first take it's light and lively; beneath the surface it's a sad search for a mate, the lament of a lonely person in search of a partner, to keep company in old age.

Loneliness in old age is omnipresent. A group of senior citizens is a poor substitute for a marriage that should have lasted years. Yet this predicament, caused by death or divorce, is a common occurrence. The contrast between a happily married couple and the request to fill out a matchmaking application is poignant. The tone is mitigated by the catchy tune, but the sadness lingers.

In "Lovely Rita," McCartney tried to pick up a meter maid for a quick fling, and almost got away with it. Such an affair is laughable. Or is it? The song merits consideration because the incongruity itself is amusing. The song's inspiration came when Paul got a parking ticket outside the Abbey Road Studios, and, when he met the female traffic warden, graciously accepted the penalty. A shallow love affair brings humorous discord to a parking ticket.

Meta Davis was the name of the warden who ticketed the Beatle. When McCartney learned Americans refer to them as meter maids,

Rita replaced Meta, and the song came to life. The Beatles performed it live for Pink Floyd on February 23, 1967 during the *Sgt. Pepper* sessions.

"Good Morning Good Morning" was inspired by a Kellogg's corn flakes commercial, that promised the "best to you each morning." It opens with a cock crowing. But instead of an optimistic message, Lennon allows the song to traverse a veritable wasteland of hopelessness. The persona wanders through town, unsure where he is going. The shops are all closed. People pass him by, and he feels needed only when a passerby asks what time it is.

The tune contains the same sense of desolation as the words, filled with foreboding. There is no hope. The singer finds no joy in his day, and the chorus of "Good morning, good morning," sounds unreal.

The persona's lack of ambition, distaste for his home life, and links with his youth portray an aimless existence. Even his past has little to offer, where nothing is new at his old school. Maybe he'll pick up a girl and go to a show. It is as if the singer is outside himself, watching his life pass by. The somnolence continues until the persona decides to go home for tea and watch *Meet the Wife*, a popular BBC sitcom.

"Good Morning Good Morning" was the closest Lennon got to put himself on the street, sensing the devastation, the wasteland of a deserted world, a twilight zone. The song is bounded by barnyard animals, from the cock crowing at the outset to the animals braying at the end. The animal sounds are arranged so each animal could be devoured or frightened by the one that precedes it, so it is an imagined chase scenario. The final sound, a chicken clucking, segues neatly into the next tune, a familiar reprise.

Pepper closes, or appears to, with the "Reprise" of the opening lines of the album. Listen closely. The "Reprise" has a faster tempo, heavier instrumentation, and is shorter than the jovial opening number. The performance is drawing to a close, and it's almost time to go.

It was Beatles assistant Neil Aspinall, who suggested the "Reprise." He reasoned if there was an opening tune, why not close the album with a farewell rendition of the same song. It gives the album a conceptual, completed, circuitous feel.

The "Reprise" serves as a bridge from "Good Morning, Good Morning" into "A Day in the Life." It marks the end of the concert and an introduction to the encore, which becomes the most potent song on the album, one which blew away every listener when they first heard it.

"A Day in the Life" is laden with portent. The fecklessness of life permeates the song. An unreal atmosphere, verging on nonsense verse, entrances the listener, even as the desperation turns one off.

"A Day in the Life" developed from the newspaper headlines recounting an automobile accident. Lennon reports the news in a monotone, after reading the *Daily Mail* of January 17, 1967. Tara Brown, a 21-year old friend of The Beatles and heir to the Guinness fortune, smashed his Lotus into a parked car when he drove through a red light. Was it a drug trip, suicide, or an accident? Leaving the meaning for the listener to fathom, Lennon plunges on. The rich and famous create an aura all their own; crowds gather for the blood and gore. Lennon's disillusion with war, with movies, with hypocrisy continues to a brief bridge.

In a completely different song, neatly spliced to become part of Lennon's piece, McCartney awakens to an alarm clock, gets up and dressed and heads off to work. The song was based on McCartney's recollection of bus rides as he commuted to the Liverpool Institute for Boys, where he met George Harrison. McCartney is breathing hard as he clambers aboard the double-decker bus, lights a smoke and falls into a trance.

Is this a joint? Is he high? Or is he dozing on the bus? The ambiguity is a tease.

We return to Lennon's languorous scene, as his voice drifts across the speakers. He read that a surveyor had counted how many potholes were in the roads of Blackburn, Lancashire, and came up with four thousand. To fill all the holes would take enough road material to fill the Albert Hall, remarked Terry Doran, a friend of The Beatles, and that line slipped into the song, concluded the album, and became history.

With that lovely salutation, *Sgt. Pepper* drew to a raucous, crescendo conclusion, as a forty-piece orchestra played increasingly higher and louder sounds for nearly a minute in the grand finale. A high-pitched sound at the end of the album, after the last song, was designed to annoy any dogs in the room when the album was played.

"A Day in the Life" was originally titled "In the Life Of." It is one of the few Beatle songs where the title does not appear in the song itself ("Tomorrow Never Knows" and" Yer Blues" are two more.) It took over thirty hours to complete "A Day in the Life," while The Beatles first album, *Please Please Me*, was recorded in ten hours.

And with that, The Beatles, as *Sgt. Pepper*, turned us on.

* * *

As young people struggled with their individual conflicts at home and abroad, they sought answers in the mystical songs of *Sgt. Pepper*, hidden meanings in the words, and tunes that were hummable. The majesty of The Beatles came through as they portrayed Sgt. Pepper's Lonely Hearts Club Band, which alluded to a Salvation Army Band. The album became all things to all people in the summer of 1967.

Even as *Sgt. Pepper* delved into despair, people found it a positive force. *Pepper* offered a chance to improve one's lot in life, make friends, and help others. It united baby-boomers who listened to it continuously through the summer and autumn of 1967. The idealization of the individual was promoted. Young people sought to take control of their lives, be someone and do something. The power of the individual was emphasized with the album.

The *Sgt. Pepper* audience, both on record and in real life, was very receptive to the message. Hippies looked at the world as a hedonistic experience. They wanted to know themselves first, and Harrison's paean met that need. Self-examination was the route to the message of love, whether through drugs, transcendental meditation, or a philosophical searching.

Message rock brought the universality of the individual onto vinyl so all the world could hear what was happening. As young people of the 1960s matured, so, too, did the songs they listened to. Thus The Beatles managed to stay on top of an evolving, aging musical audience by writing and recording topical tunes.

Pepper initiated an interest in the life of India and the culture of the East, from philosophies to religions to music. The Beatles forged a new type of musical album, laden with intricate design and hidden humor.

Sgt. Pepper was the culmination of the sense of despair that crystallized in *Revolver*. *Pepper* gave birth to an era of universal love, adopted by the hippie generation as their own. Meditation flourished. Indian music and culture grew popular in the West. The individual assumed an expanded role.

The rebirth of The Beatles through *Sgt. Pepper* was an act of self-realization. It sounded the death knell to the loneliness of the outside world. As performers who no longer performed, The Beatles withdrew even as they forged a new direction to pursue their music.

Could The Beatles surpass their magnum opus?

Nothing else they ever recorded approached the majesty of

Pepper. Maybe it was the time of year, or the time of man. Maybe it was the record itself, but the generation in search of itself believed The Beatles recorded their best album with *Sgt. Pepper*.

Sgt. Pepper remains the all time best-selling album in Great Britain, and number six in the States.

* * *

Anthony Costello (retired psychiatrist) was living in a small flat in England, the smallest house around. *"I remember the neighbors came rushing up the stairs and burst into our flat. Come on, you have to listen to this. It's The Beatles' newest album, Sgt. Pepper."* Anthony admits he wasn't really into pop music at the time, but recalls that announcement as clear as day.

Betsy Dripps (teacher) used to teach school in Pennsylvania and recalls a little boy whose surname was Pepper. *"They called him Sergeant. Wonder where he is today. He'd be 36 years old, so it was right around that era."* Like many of us, Betsy still has her collection of Beatle albums in tact.

Shelley Christiansen (writer/realtor): *"They played **Sgt. Pepper** in my dorm all the time when I was a freshman at Syracuse University. Played it over and over, so much that I learned all the words by heart and never had to buy the album. I used to walk down the hall, and one room would have 'Lucy in the Sky' and another was playing 'Fixing a Hole.' And I was going through a growing up phase, just as The Beatles were going through a musical transition of their own."*

Anna Marie D'Addarie (administrative assistant): *"I can't believe it was 40 years ago. I'm so incredibly old. I remember the night the album came out. I was a junior in high school, and my friend, my rich friend, got the* album. *And we were in her basement, and it was totally cool. I was a good Catholic girl and one of the six of us brought a joint, a single joint. And listening to* **Sgt. Pepper**, *that was the one and only time I smoked. I was a cheerleader, a good Catholic girl.*

"I remember everything from that evening. We must have listened to the album a million times, and didn't understand a word. The album just made that moment gel for me, all of that. I even listened to it backwards, because, you know, my rich friend had a turntable you could play backwards."

Valerie Sonnenthal (photographer): *"I was too young for real* **Sgt. Pepper** *memories, though I thought the album cover was really cool! I am sure my brother bought it on the day of release. Funny I can't remember where he bought records."*

Maureen Hourihan (writer): *"I was twelve, and my girlfriend and I had a girls band in her basement. We thought we were really cool. I remember her older brother Kevin was 17, and he had all The Beatles albums, and we used to listen to* **Sgt. Pepper** *that summer."*

Francine Kelly (executive director): *"My baby-sitter sold our* **Sgt. Pepper** *album on the black market. We were in Turkey, and he got deported back to the States when they found out what he'd done. He stole all our albums and sold them in Turkey. The US Government sent his family home to avoid prosecution by the Turkish authorities. That's my memory of* **Sgt. Pepper**.*"*

Ann Marie Reid (registered nurse): *"It was a big deal; it's one of the best albums ever. I actually replaced my album with a CD. I was just a little girl, born in 1958. We had a console record player in the dining room. My parents listened to Ray Coniff and those singers. I was only eight, but my cousins were in their mid to late teens, and they left us four Beatles albums. I still have them. We would just play them over and over. It was such a change in what they'd done. I said, 'This is unbelievable. Who is Billy Shears?' I kept staring at the* cover, at all those people's heads. I remember one Easter when it was snowy and we just listened to **Sgt. Pepper** over and over. It was all happy, all good."

Jim Athearn (farm manager): *"I spend a lot of time with young people. And very often I find they love Beatles music and we can listen to it together."* He goes on: *"I remember every time The Beatles came out with a new song, you knew it would be great. But you had to listen a couple of times to get a comfort level with it. It was such a leap from 'I Want to Hold Your Hand' to 'Lucy in the Sky with Diamonds.'"* And he adds, *"I do remember feeling the need to adjust to something new."*

Sam Feldman (not-for-profit board member): *"Sure I remember* **Sgt. Pepper***. It was fun. It was a good time."*

Kathleen Forsythe (graphic designer): *"It was the greatest album ever."*

Susie Marsh (graphic designer) had just graduated from high school in Washington, D.C. She remembers going to a Be-In in Manhattan. She bought some clothing ornaments, flat on one side and faceted on the other, glass crystals. *"I used telephone wire to wrap the crystals together, and I wore them as wire-rim glasses so I could look like John Lennon. It was like looking through a kaleidoscope. I loved* **Sgt. Pepper***."*
She adds, *"Thirty-three years later I had the amazing experience of working with Paul McCartney when I designed his book,* **Paul McCartney: Paintings** *for Bullfinch Press. He was just the way I had always imagined him—joyously enthusiastic about making music, still cute, and a little goofy."*

Vitaly Sokolovsky (test engineer) was in Minsk. *"I heard it on reel-to-reel tapes through friends. It took a while to get it. It was on the radio. There was no easy access. You needed friends, just like in the song. We heard The Beatles on the short-wave radio. You had to sift through the rumors, and pass* the music under the table. It was quite an investigation. We never had the album in Russia. We had to find someone to make a copy."

His wife Elina adds: *"We wanted to see the cover, to see if they really had a picture of Marx or Lenin. And when we finally saw it, they dressed so funny."*

Vitaly adds: *"I remember when I heard the "Reprise," of the first song again, I thought to myself, can they do that?"* Of course it was The Beatles, and they could. And did.

Alan Degutis (antiquarian librarian): *"Glad to hear that you're finding that the sixties aren't so bad after all! I enjoyed the sixties myself, though back in the sixties I didn't spend much time thinking about the time when I'd be in* **my** *sixties. You're taking a more personal approach to The Beatles' impact on you and our generation, right?*

"Let's not forget that 1967 was also the year of the Impossible Dream...Yaz, Jim Lonborg, Dick Williams and company. I don't know whether music or baseball has changed more in the last forty years.... No doubt we've changed, too, and see the past through rose-colored lenses. It doesn't seem like forty years have gone by since **Sgt. Pepper** *came out.*

"One thing I remember...hearing **Sgt. Pepper** *at your house on Manning Street was part of what led to our buying a new record player. We had gotten the album (that goes without saying) and I'd listened to it a number of times (that, too, goes without saying). But I then heard it at your house (the room with the ping-pong table) and was stunned at how much more detail I was hearing for the first time. I believe we had a small monaural record player at the time. It was suddenly clear that it wasn't adequate for the new sonic dimensions The Beatles were exploring. Of course, in those days, deciding you needed a new stereo and actually getting one were two different matters.*

"When the **Magical Mystery Tour** *album came out, available in stereo only, that really pushed things over the edge. (Remember how, before that time, albums were available in mono and in stereo, the latter usually a dollar or so more?) When Capitol (and other labels) stopped making mono albums, it was*

definitely time to get a stereo, and we did. I think we bought it at Holden TV on Main St. (long gone, as are many of the establishments of that era).
   "*So many good memories of those days.*"

My brother **Richard Dresser (playwrite)** wrote of the 40th anniversary celebration of *Sgt. Pepper*. "*This sounds like quite an event brewing on the Vineyard. I'm sure it will touch a lot of people and trigger an avalanche of memories.*"

The Boston Globe of March 30, 2007 recounted the memories of a Vietnam vet who was in the Navy, stationed at the Mekong Delta. His recollection of listening to the album on a record player linger to this day. "*It was a moment I will never forget, and every time I hear a song from that album it brings me back to the evening, sitting in a small compartment on our ship in the middle of the Run Sat River, listening to music that took us to a far different place in time.*" He didn't leave his name, other than Vet Guest, only his memories. He added, "*Being in the situation we were in, the album 'brought us back home' to what our contemporaries were listening to in the states.*"

Scott Campbell (art teacher): "*My high school friend and I agreed to meet in the year 2000, to reminisce—I still have a sealed copy of the original mono—not stereo record that was out just before the stereo one was minted in 1966(?). I bought it just before my buddy Jeff Martin went off to Vietnam to fight as a Marine.*
   "*We agreed to open it when he came back.*
   "*He never came back.*
   "*I am as opposed to wars of any kind today as I was then.*"

* * *

Three weeks after *Sgt. Pepper* was released, The Beatles went public on *Our World*, a televised concert broadcast live from Britain into 26 countries around the world. John Lennon wrote and The Beatles recorded a masterpiece in two weeks, one of their fastest accomplishments, then auditioned the anthem for the live concert. It was entitled "All You Need is Love." On June 25, 1967, The Beatles sang their mantra to an international audience estimated at 350 million people.

The simple refrain delivered the basic theme of the universality of love. It was a perfect *Pepper* postscript. The song was dedicated to the love generation and offered hope to everyone under the inclusive mantle of love. It is a song of hope, of people revitalizing themselves. The message is that each of us has the potential to be someone special. This is our chance.

"All You Need is Love" opens with *Le Marseillaise* and includes snippets of Bach, Glenn Miller's "In the Mood," and John and Paul reprising the yeah-yeah-yeahs of "She Loves You." Lennon kept the lyrics simple to increase international comprehension. The music is easy to hum, and the basic chorus transcends generations and cultures.

John Lennon was keen on creating slogans that united people. This was one of his most universal efforts. Indeed, it was voted the favorite song in England and played to welcome Queen Elizabeth into the Millenium Dome on December 31, 1999 and again at her golden jubilee in June 2002. At the last occasion, however, "God Save the Queen" replaced" Le Marseillaise" in the introduction.

(In a much less auspicious event in 2007, the song was used in a commercial to sell diapers, with the words, "All you need is Luvs.")

The flip side of the single that emerged from the concert was "Baby You're a Rich Man." Like "A Day in the Life," this was a mix of the masters. John was working on a song, tentatively titled "One of the Beautiful People." Paul had the basics for "Baby You're a Rich Man." Under the auspices of George Martin, they merged the two sections into one song, with the emphasis on things that matter rather than dependence on money. Mick Jagger was credited with singing in the chorus. The Beatles utilized a primitive synthesizer, known as a clavioline, an amplified keyboard, to create unusual sounds. The song was aimed at beautiful people and asks rhetorical questions, while The Beatles respond with deft answers as they ape their role as rich rock stars.

* * *

Throughout their remarkable career The Beatles constantly challenged themselves. Their songs were personal, yet shared common feelings with an eager audience. The link between singer and audience fueled a kinship where fans felt part of The Beatles' world. It was the epitome of rock music.

The message The Beatles promulgated was intended—and indeed became—an antidote to the loneliness in the world around them. *Sgt. Pepper* was the most creative, advanced, perfected work The Beatles ever produced. With *Pepper* they realized much more than their potential. No one, not even The Beatles themselves, would ever approach the majesty that was *Pepper*, even when they took a Magical Mystery Tour.

McCartney says *Pepper* was an attempt to stand outside The Beatles, to take on another persona, to become someone different. It was an experiment, one that could never be replicated. It stood on its own, a shining star in the universe of pop music.

* * *

Toward the end of August 1967, amid the fervor of *Sgt. Pepper*, Brian Epstein, the clever businessman who discovered The Beatles and steered them to a road of fame and fortune, took his life. It was sad that a man who did so much for so many, did not appreciate the value of his own life. The Beatles learned of his death as they embarked on a trip to Wales under the auspices of the Maharishi Mahesh Yogi.

* * *

Another record, released in the autumn of 1967 was their second double-A single of the year, with McCartney's "Hello Goodbye" on one side and Lennon's "I Am the Walrus" on the other. This record is in profound contrast to the "Penny Lane/Strawberry Fields Forever" piece six months earlier. Neither song is emblematic of the era and both have limited appeal.

"Hello Goodbye" is an updated version of "We Can Work It Out." Paul, as the eternal optimist, kept the theme of tranquility alive with "Hello Goodbye." The song is a contradiction, a string of opposites, of all the possibilities we have. McCartney dashed it off, listing ups and downs of life. The original title for the tune was "Hello Hello."

It was released in November 1967, in time for Christmas. It became a Beatles Christmas hit, holding the top position for seven weeks. The false ending, dead air, and return of the song were a challenge for DJs, although the popularity of the song quickly won them over. (The song was later used by Target, with the revised title, "Hello, Good Buy.")

John Lennon felt he was relegated to the B side of the single as he countered with a musical nonsense song, psychedelic rock with obtuse lyrics, written in response to Dylan's "Rainy Day Women #12" and "35." Lennon's words were laden obtuse meaning and ominous tones, but made a great song.

"I am the Walrus" is actually an amalgam of three unfinished songs in Lennon's library. One revolved around a police siren he heard near his house, which prompted the line about the policemen;

another was based on misty impressions of his garden in the rain; and the third, the nonsense verse about a cornflake, was an extension of the inspiration for "Good Morning, Good Morning," but designed intentionally to confuse and amuse his fans.

A reason for the nonsense lyrics allegedly originated from a letter Lennon received from his alma mater, the Quarry Bank Grammar School. A student mentioned his teacher assigned the class a lesson that required them to analyze Beatles lyrics. Lennon was intrigued enough to add a few nonsense lines, to intrigue the teacher, students, and fans.

While Lennon claims in song to be the Walrus, in a later tune, "Glass Onion," he assigned Paul that role. The Walrus was lifted from Lewis Carroll's poem "The Walrus and the Carpenter" in *Through the Looking Glass*. Lennon didn't realize he should have sided with the better creature, the Carpenter, not the Walrus. Too late.

Semolina Pilchard referred to Detective Sergeant Norman Pilcher of Scotland Yard, who later arrested John on drug possession. Still later, Pilcher was charged with blackmail and bribery. What goes around comes around.

"I Am the Walrus" closes with lines by Sir John Gielgud from Shakespeare's *King Lear*, on the death of Oswald in Act IV Scene VI, recorded off the BBC in a radio play. The point is pointless, but the wordplay is magnificent.

* * *

Magical Mystery Tour

I sit in a red velvet chair at Roger Gale's Beacon Street apartment. He has a new set of headphones and just bought the album, **Magical Mystery Tour.** *He hooks me up, and I plunge right into the music. It is a powerful* *experience, though I feel it does not quite live up to* **Sgt. Pepper**. *For one thing, I already know all the songs on the second side.*

Standing on the corner of Tremont and Boylston Streets in downtown Boston, I gaze up at the marquee of a movie theatre. The words **Magical Mystery Tour** *stare back at me. I really want to see the movie, but I want my girlfriend to join me. She can't. By the next day, the film has been pulled from the theatre. It was years before I saw it.*

I spend a night in my car in Detroit in March of 1968, too cheap to get a hotel room, unaware how cold the night would be. The only thing that keeps me warm is whenever I turn on the car to warm up, "Lady Madonna" sings to me on the radio. It is a memorable evening.

I drive a girl, Rebecca Mobile, home from BU in the spring 1968. We come to Holden for dinner and meet the family, then I take her back to West Haven Connecticut. I want to return in time to see the New York launch of Apple Corps by John and Paul. I make it, barely, and witness my boys go into business.

During the summer of 1968, I drive cross-country with a couple of girls and land in Berkeley, California, the night Bobby Kennedy is assassinated. We listen to Procol Harem's "Whiter Shade of Pale" over and over that night. Somehow the music calms our anguish.

I venture through Haight Ashbury. Word is that George Harrison visited the Haight, wearing heart-shaped sunglasses. I never see him, but it is exciting to know he was in town.

I first hear "Hey Jude" in late August 1968. My girlfriend Maureen is in a group planning to climb Mt. Washington. I go along for the ride, sitting in the backseat, Maureen on my lap, as we drive along, listening to "Hey Jude" on the radio. The song awes me.

My friend John Zielin and I crowd into the Sherman Union to watch The Beatles sing "Hey Jude" on the **Smothers Brothers Show**. *The room is spellbound. The Beatles have done it again.*

"Pride can hurt you, too," was an admonition The Beatles issued on "She Loves You," way back in 1964. The warning returned to haunt them in their efforts to follow the triumph of *Sgt. Pepper*. The sense was that The Beatles could do no wrong in the rock music world, but, unfortunately, they proved their public wrong.

Having mastered popular music, John, Paul, George, and Ringo sought a new medium to demonstrate their talents. Two ventures they attempted in the post-*Pepper* era, however, never came to fruition the way they were envisioned.

The Beatles made a movie, by themselves, entitled *Magical Mystery Tour*. It was deemed a failure from the moment it was released on the BBC, in black and white, in London on Boxing Day, the day after Christmas, 1967. Reviewers of the premier were smug in their criticism that The Beatles had met disaster. Finally.

And not long after the *Magical Mystery Tour* miasma, The Beatles tried their hand in business, and again stumbled. Apple Corps was designed to support struggling artists, but was mismanaged and faltered almost before it was launched. A sideline of a clothing store ended up as a massive giveaway.

Perhaps it was the heady success following *Pepper*. Maybe The Beatles had made their mark in music and should have been content with that. Whatever the root of their traumas, the failures in film and retail business taught John and Paul that they were not invincible. Their talents as a musicians were unquestioned, but attempts to enter other markets were not met with similar success.

* * *

Magical Mystery Tour was a homemade-videotaped movie. Paul McCartney directed it, with the intention to let the spirit of the moment dictate the plot. He saw it as an extension of Ken Kesey and the Merry Pranksters on their magic bus as chronicled in Tom Wolfe's The Electric Kool-Aid Acid Test. The Beatles cavorted through the English countryside, movie cameras in hand, filming whatever activity or inaction they choose to create. The movie never got off the ground, though The Beatles made amusing attempts to bring film and music together. Without a story line, there was no story. However, in later years it has made great late-night viewing for an audience intrigued with cutting-edge film. For professionals, it should never have been removed from the film canister.

In England, the movie songs were packaged in two EP (extended play) records: *Magical Mystery Tour, Fool on the Hill, Blue Jay Way* and *Your Mother Should Know*. Words and stills were included in a booklet, which actually sold quite well. But it wasn't *Sgt. Pepper*. Once the fiasco of the film, *Magical Mystery Tour*, wore off, the songs faded into a forgotten reservoir of Beatles singles.

In the States, Capital Records sought a more receptive audience. Broadening the EP format, and including six previously released singles, *Magical Mystery Tour* was released as an album in November 1967, a month prior to the movie's debut. To follow *Sgt. Pepper* was daunting. The album *Magical Mystery Tour* is gaudy and gauche. Compared to *Sgt. Pepper*, it is a pretentious effort that belied the professional skills of the Beatles. It sold well because *Sgt. Pepper* had raised expectations, and the movie had not yet been released.

Magical Mystery Tour was an indication that the summer of love had faded into an autumn of dismay.

The album *Magical Mystery Tour* is as an egocentric pat on the back from The Beatles to themselves. It didn't make it, although it captures the essence of the historic post-*Pepper* atmosphere of 1967, including all the signature songs of the era, from "Penny Lane" and "Strawberry Fields" through "All You Need is Love" and "I am the Walrus."

The Beatles made no attempt at a common theme in *Magical Mystery Tour*. Capitol Records simply dished out a collection of singles. The possibility for a theme was evident with the opening bars of the first song, yet it never came together as a cohesive album;

it was only the extended-play, four-song set in Great Britain. From the time they recorded the opening song it was five months before they filmed the movie. Unlike *Pepper*, beyond these welcoming lines, nothing bound the album together.

Magical Mystery Tour, the title song of the album, set the welcoming nature of the adventure about to unfold. In the sixties, in Britain, bus trips to undisclosed locations were popular. What could be more fun than a bus ride with The Beatles! Unfortunately, filming of the project was poorly managed, undisciplined, and without the benefit of a director, so the project foundered, although in retrospect it engenders a culturally artistic appeal.

"Fool on the Hill" chastises the silly people who pop up in Beatle songs from "Eleanor Rigby" through "Lady Madonna." The fool could be the Maharishi, the Indian sage The Beatles followed. Many people considered him a fool, with his hollow, immature laugh. The fool on the hill holds knowledge, hope, and help for mankind. "Fool on the Hill" is McCartney's take on Lennon's "Nowhere Man."

The inspiration for the song allegedly was derived from an incident with Martha, Paul's sheepdog. He was walking her one morning on Primrose Hill, admiring the beauty of the landscape. Martha went missing. As Paul was looking around, a man suddenly appeared, with Martha. Paul thanked him. When Paul turned, the man vanished. Paul spent the day trying to figure out what had happened. To make the case more mysterious, Paul had been discussing the role of God with his friend Alistair Taylor. Was this a visit from the big man?

The third song on the *Mystery Tour* has no lyrics. It was one of the few songs credited to all four Beatles, and began as a jam session. The Beatles used a mellotron and began to chant at the end. The impression is an uplifting, escapist atmosphere. Originally titled "Aerial Tour Instrumental," "Flying" soars along for just over two minutes, although the original recording was nine minutes long.

"Flying" could have had lyrics, but it fit nicely as a bridge into George Harrison's "Blue Jay Way."

"Blue Jay Way" is a vacuous account of Harrison's experience waiting for his friend Derek Taylor. George was in a rented house on Blue Jay Way in Hollywood Hills, with a panoramic view of Los Angeles. Impatient that Taylor was late, Harrison sat down and wrote a song about waiting. The chorus line, asking him to not be so late, was repeated twenty-nine times.

"Blue Jay Way" spoke to a confusion in directions. More likely it was Harrison's allegory to discover more about himself, and his fans finding their way through the mysteries and miseries of life. The mantra, "Don't be long," can be taken as "Don't belong," which adds another dimension. The song meanders, as someone who is unsure, stumbles along.

McCartney's "Your Mother Should Know" reverts to the "When I'm 64" style of a hurdy-gurdy piano piece, bouncing along. It has a catchy beat, but the repetitive lyrics don't take it far enough. McCartney wrote the song for the final scene in the movie, *Magical Mystery Tour*, when The Beatles parade down the grand staircase. The most memorable moment of that scene was that John, George, and Ringo wore red carnations; Paul's carnation was black, which fueled the "Paul is dead" rumor.

The album has a few good songs, but none of the caliber of *Pepper*. The movie, *Magical Mystery Tour*, opened in the States, was shown for a few days, harshly panned, then abruptly yanked. Admittedly an amateur effort, in later years critics favored it with more respect. (It was nowhere to be seen until re-released in 1976.)

*   *   *

As quickly as The Beatles embarked on their Magical Mystery Tour, they jumped into another venture, a mysterious miasma that exhibited an inept sense of business. Their marketing acumen was all off.

The Apple Boutique opened on London's Baker Street on December 5, 1967, hosting trinkets and clothes from around the world. Psychedelic clothes on the racks made a dramatic display. It was rumored there might even be a Beatle behind the cash register. There was no financial planning, no marketing, and within eight months, The Beatles abandoned the retail store and gave away $25,000 worth of merchandise.

When they succeeded, they were stupendous; when they failed, it was a disaster.

Back in the recording studio in February 1968, The Beatles recorded several songs that found their way onto various albums, but they had no coherent road map to follow. They had done it all and now didn't know which way to go.

The first song The Beatles released in 1968 was McCartney's "Lady Madonna," a lively tribute to Mary, the mother of Christ or a prostitute, take your pick. Paul claimed he wrote the song for all women, everywhere. John added the line about seeing how they run, which had been part of his "I am the Walrus." The song includes all the days of the week with the exception of Saturday.

"Lady Madonna" represented a return to the black-inspired soul music that fascinated The Beatles, back in the late-1950s. The beat and brassiness of the song recall the sound of Fats Domino. Indeed, the New Orleans jazz singer recorded the song later in 1968 and it was a hit. "Lady Madonna" was the first clue The Beatles were about to embark in another direction, a return to their roots.

The flip side of "Lady Madonna" was George Harrison's "Inner Light," which introduced Indian music into western pop culture. Harrison went beyond "Nowhere Man" and "Fool on the Hill" to describe an all-knowing sage who sees all, hears everything, yet is aloof from the petty pressures and distractions of people around him. The song champions the virtues of contentment within, akin to the theme of Harrison's "Within You Without You."

"Inner Light" was the first George Harrison tune on a Beatles single. The song only appeared on an album in the States in 1980 on *The Beatles' Rarities*. Indian musicians were employed to record the instrumental track in Bombay, India. The words were translated from Tao Te Ching in the foundation book of Daoism. "Inner Light" was the last time Harrison incorporated Indian music into a Beatle song.

Just as McCartney traveled back to the roots of rock with "Lady Madonna," Harrison traversed the continents to incorporate Indian ragas into Beatle music. And as The Beatles were about to embark on a trip to India, "Inner Light" illuminated the way.

But first The Beatles had another movie in the works.

* * *

Yellow Submarine

Yellow Submarine was a cartoon in which The Beatles were reduced to mere characterizations of themselves, engaged in a struggle to ward off the Blue Meanies and protect Pepperland. *Yellow Submarine* was intended to be a children's movie, stepping into a new market for the lads from Liverpool. And the movie provided a vehicle for The Beatles to promote new songs, and include a few old releases.

The single, "Yellow Submarine" was released in August 1966; the movie *Yellow Submarine* came out in the autumn of 1968, and the soundtrack album debuted in January 1969.

The Beatles appeared as themselves in the closing scene of *Yellow Submarine*, lending a humorous spoof to the enterprise. Although the movie had been completed, the album took months to reach the records stores. It was a marketing management move, which showed that The Beatles, running Apple Corps, did not have all the skills necessary to capture promotion as they should have. With their name on the film, and later the album, that proved sufficient to reach successful sales. The movie was a hit.

The album *Yellow Submarine* was produced in a manner similar to *Mystery Tour* in that it was a collection of a few new songs from the film and several old retreads. The title track was written by Paul McCartney in 1966 for *Revolver*, as a children's song; it was the B side to the single "Eleanor Rigby."

The story is cheerful, though a little ominous, and tells the story of a captain of a submarine. Listen carefully to "Yellow Submarine," with its vibrant tune. Background sounds and screeches add palpable excitement. The urgent blast of a boat's whistle, sailors dashing to their positions, and the calm that follows the emergency, are part of the song. Ringo played harmonica. George swirled water in a bucket for ocean sounds and John blew bubbles with a straw. Donovan Leach was part of the studio staff who helped with attendant noises.

The song earned the Ivor Novello Award for the best-selling single in the UK in 1966, but did not fare as well in the States, perhaps due to Lennon's bigger-than-Jesus comments at the time it was released. The song is alleged to refer to Nebutal capsules, which are hypnotic, but McCartney denied the accusation. Shortly after the song was released, a yellow barbiturate was christened a yellow submarine.

Another children's song on the *Yellow Submarine* album is "All Together Now." This simplistic tune, addressed to the *Sesame Street* set, teaches counting, the alphabet, and color names. The song simplifies growing up, but retains a hummable tune and a beat, the trademark of many a Beatle song.

It is composed in a skiffle style, with a simple background. A car horn appears at the end of this children's ditty. (The song is sung at football games in the UK and served as the basis for a Verizon telephone ad in 2002.)

"Hey Bulldog" has a threatening tone, with adult preaching, which stands in sharp juxtaposition to the infantile tenets of "All Together Now." John started the song as "Hey Bullfrog," but Paul started to bark, so the song became "Hey Bulldog," although there is nothing in the lyrics that refers to dogs. Another working title for the tune was "You Can Talk to Me". The informal chatter and laughter in the background add to the flavor of the song. John and Paul banter and bark back and forth. This song was recorded while The Beatles were finishing up "Lady Madonna." It was the first time John brought Yoko to one of The Beatles recording sessions, and it was the last song The Beatles recorded before their trip to India.

George Harrison had a pair of contributions to *Yellow Submarine*. "It's All Too Much" was recorded during the *Pepper* sessions, probably intended to be included with *Magical Mystery Tour*, but was held back, in part because of its length, over six minutes. At the time, it was the longest song The Beatles had recorded. Harrison's admonitions encompass diet and teatime, and in writing to children, he makes his points succinctly.

"Only a Northern Song" is limited, neither intellectually nor culturally stimulating. The message is simple, the theme repetitive, and the style immature. The song belittles itself, as it refers either to Liverpool, a city in the north of England or Northern Songs, the company that handled the compositions of John and Paul. It also belittles George himself when he acts as if it doesn't matter what he plays or sings; it's only a northern song.

As background, an argument had ensued over Northern Songs. NEMS was the name of Brian Epstein's music business. Following his untimely death, after the release of *Sgt. Pepper* in the summer of 1967, copyright restrictions impeded The Beatles. Northern Songs

Ltd. was the publishing company that copyrighted Beatle songs prior to the creation of Apple Corps. Hence Harrison's lament.

(In the 1970s, a lawsuit was filed against George Harrison for plagiarism in his masterpiece "My Sweet Love." He responded with "This Song," a similar invective which addressed his songwriting tribulations.)

"Only a Northern Song" was recorded in February 1967, and intended for *Sgt. Pepper*, but The Beatles felt the content and style conflicted with the *Pepper* theme. Hence, it too, was held back, and released as part of *Yellow Submarine*.

* * *

Yellow Submarine, released late in 1968, concluded with the anthem "All You Need is Love," universally accepted as a trademark Beatle song, the theme for the summer of love, the epitome of the *Sgt. Pepper* era, and an innocent song which easily meshes with a children's album. That's the first side of the *Yellow Submarine* album.

The flip side of *Yellow Submarine* is a selection of musical compositions by producer George Martin, "the fifth Beatle." Martin's harmonic pieces provide a soothing background for the movie *Yellow Submarine*, and make easy listening in contrast to The Beatles somewhat disjointed musical selections. The electronic background music for the second side of *Yellow Submarine* was recorded in 1968.

* * *

The Beatles were about to set off for India, intent on garnering new wisdom from a guru who taught them to look within to escape the stress of daily life. This theory evolved into Transcendental Meditation or TM.

The Beatles were not the only ones interested in the guru, Maharishi Yogi. The Beach Boys, Mia Farrow and her sister Prudence, and Donovan accompanied them to Rishikesh, India, in the winter of 1968. The motivation for the trip had been sparked the previous summer when The Beatles attended a lecture by the Maharishi. They were bound for a retreat with him in Wales when they learned their manager had died. The Maharishi used that event to steer The Beatles toward TM to cope with Brian Epstein's suicide.

The Beatles had high expectations for Transcendental Meditation. Yet, the experience in India proved a step down the road of dissolution for the band.

As young men from Liverpool, they did not take to the unusual tastes of Indian life. Ringo found the food too spicy, and left Rishikesh after little more than a week. Paul and Jane Asher soon followed. John and George stuck it out nearly three months, until John discovered some un-holy intentions emanating from the Maharishi toward Mia Farrow. Lennon quickly and angrily grew disillusioned, convinced George, and they left in a huff. George, however, continued to find peace through meditation and appreciated the influence of the Maharishi in his music for the rest of his life.

The trip to India proved productive in the musical sense. While on sabbatical from the tumult of the London music scene, The Beatles composed more than thirty tunes, many quite engaging and uplifting. And on their return from India, they found they had evolved well beyond the happy-go-lucky band of *Sgt. Pepper*.

John Lennon grew restless. Paul McCartney wanted to settle down and raise a family. George Harrison was inspired to pursue Indian philosophy and music. Ringo Starr had his eyes on Hollywood. The Beatles realized their magical mystery tour to India had changed them more than they could imagine, and the cohesion of the group had fragmented.

But they still had more music to make.

* * *

Back in London in the spring of 1968 they sought to regain control of their musical and business empire. The musical angle of Apple Corps was desperate for direction. Paul and George grew deeply involved in the promotion of budding musicians. Among their newfound stars were Mary Hopkin, James Taylor, Billy Preston, and the Apple band Badfinger.

But there were more than musicians. Groupies and hangers-on clogged Apple's corridors with irrelevant or self-serving business ventures. Money poured out of the coffers like wine. The Beatles stood back as their empire struggled to gain footing. No one took charge. Scammers took advantage of The Beatles financially, pilfering the profits, something Brian Epstein would never have tolerated.

When they flew into New York City in May 1968, John Lennon and Paul McCartney addressed Wall Street in an effort to promote their new entry into the business world. They determined Apple Corps would enter with a flashy appearance, so they chartered a Chinese junk for press reports, appeared on television for interviews and were very open with the announcement that Apple Corps would be a haven for the undiscovered artist, a bastion of new recordings and avant-garde music. They garnered publicity and raised expectations with lofty promises which could not be fulfilled.

And The Beatles had personal issues to resolve, even as they created a business monster beyond their ken. John's marriage to Cynthia dissolved as he fell under the spell of Yoko Ono, a Japanese artist and sometime musician. He was drawn to her unique sense of humor in art: a sign on an apple with a price of 200 pounds and the offer to watch the apple rot; a tiny telescope at the top of ladder; when you peek inside you see the word 'yes'. John and Yoko moved in together, and too soon Yoko showed up at recording sessions. John had found his partner in love, but Yoko's presence was a decided drain on the energy of the other Beatles.

In the spring of 1968 Paul McCartney, age 26, was still unmarried. Next to Prince Charles, he was England's most eligible bachelor. And Paul was anxious to settle down. Jane Asher refused to sacrifice her acting career to marry a Beatle, so Paul looked elsewhere. Photographer Linda Eastman, from Scarsdale New York, the same town Yoko Ono had lived in, sought Paul out, and they quickly became an item, below the radar. Paul and Linda's relationship was very private; the public really only became aware of their rapport when they were married in March 1969.

George and Ringo worked on their own marriages in 1968. George was drawn into the TM movement and studied Indian philosophy. He learned to play a number of Indian instruments and studied the music. Patti Boyd was apparently happy, although their marriage was not to last. Ringo played the role of the family man with his son Zak, and tested the waters of Hollywood. His marriage was stable, for now.

Through the early summer of 1968 rumors spread that The Beatles had broken up. Other stories had them recording four separate albums, that there was anger in the recording studio and discord in Pepperland. Change is hard. Without the firm hand of a manager, The Beatles lacked direction and cohesion. The trip to India expanded their world view but accented their differences. Just as *Magical Mystery Tour* flopped as a movie, Apple Corps could not sustain the fractured management style and laissez-faire attitude. And The Beatles were growing up. In 1968 John and Ringo both turned 28.

The very public love affair between John and Yoko could not be ignored. Yoko sought recognition for her work, and some say she used John and The Beatles to promote herself. Yet she did inspire him, and he, in turn, tried to get his fans behind Yoko. Even as John gained attention, he lost respect.

White art was John and Yoko's thing. They dressed in white. They painted white canvases and set balloons free. They planted acorns for peace on the grounds of Liverpool's Coventry Cathedral. John and Yoko became public exhibitionists of their newfound love, with front and rear nude photographs which adorned the album of sound they created that first night they got together in May 1968. Two Virgins garnered notoriety based on the reputation of its cover, rather than the music within the sleeves. Such a public display of unclothed affection offended a segment of Beatle fans. Although Two Virgins was wrapped in brown paper, it still alienated many people, including the rest of the band. Now John and Yoko faced hostility from The Beatles themselves, as well as their public.

Paul, George, and Ringo grew dismayed by John's activities. Since he had fallen for Yoko, Apple Corps and The Beatles were no longer the primary focus of his life. Paul resented Yoko's presence and John's preoccupation with her. Paul felt the future of The Beatles was at stake if John continued down this dogma of disconnect.

Paul directed The Beatles through their subsequent albums. While he had been the de facto creator of *Sgt. Pepper*, he now became the catalyst for The Beatles' subsequent work.

Paul composed *Hey Jude*, the biggest selling single The Beatles ever sang. Recorded in mid-summer 1968, the song stretches out over seven minutes. When producer George Martin said The Beatles could never produce a song that long, John looked at him and said, "We can. We're The Beatles. We can do anything." That sense of bravado never died, even when his heart was elsewhere.

"Hey Jude" was written in sympathy for Julian, the son John abandoned when he took up with Yoko. The original title was "Hey Jules." Paul was around during John and Cynthia's divorce and wanted to do something to cheer up Julian. (Ironically, it was twenty years before Julian learned the song had actually been written for him.) John thought Paul wrote the song to him, and Paul said he'd written it to himself. But it was for Julian.

For nine weeks, "Hey Jude" enjoyed the number-one slot in the States. It proved the most commercially successful Beatles single of all time. At seven minutes eleven seconds, it was the longest single ever to reach number one. And as the first release for Apple Corps it was the best debut single for a new record company. The song opens with a single instrument and builds to a crescendo of fifty. The fade out lasts four minutes; the chorus is repeated nineteen times.

Assumptions have been made that *Jude* is a religious reference, a cocaine high, or a singer's lament. The ambiguity leant intrigue to all suppositions and boosted record sales.

There was ambiguity as well on the flip side of the record, Lennon's paean "Revolution," a brash, bold statement on how to change the world. He was first moved to compose the song in the spring of 1968 when French students rioted against their government. Later, he slowed the speed of the song, and it was released as the mayhem of the Democratic convention was televised around the world in August of 1968.

It is remarkable that in the summer of 1967 "All You Need is Love" was the key song, and merely a year later, "Revolution" was on everyone's lips. The song spoke directly to political protestors all around the world, with active talk of revolution, protests, demonstrations and moratoriums against the war in Vietnam. Lennon sought a peaceful plan for change, but let his animosity toward war and "the establishment" spew forth in the words to "Revolution."

(Ironically "Revolution" was the first Beatles song used in advertising. When Nike manipulated use of it in 1987, there was a backlash against use of Beatles music in commercial ventures.)

The song opens with a searing guitar, a crashing drum and a scream that demands attention. Some have theorized this song presaged heavy-metal rock.

As the first single from Apple Corp, The Beatles set the bar high. Adding a touch of class, they sent their debut single "Hey Jude"/ "Revolution" to the Queen, along with three singles from Apple recording artists, entitled, "Our First Four." Queen Elizabeth responded that she was, "greatly touched by this kind thought from The Beatles."

The week of August 11-18, 1968 was proclaimed National Apple Week by The Beatles, and "Hey Jude" proved a runaway bestseller. The flip side did much to ensure there were sounds of "Revolution" in the streets.

* * *

Judy Case (therapeutic recreation director): *"Their songs provided the perfect backdrop to my coming-of-age years. As their music grew and changed, so did I. Each unique song evoked a memory from those turbulent, fun, fabulous years.*

"'Love Me Do'—a naive young teen madly in love with all four of them, my favorite changing daily (or was it the hair I loved?) 'We Can Work It Out'— can my boyfriend and I? (We didn't). 'Revolution'—does John suggest violence or non-violence? 'I Am The Walrus'—sitting in the pizza parlor trying to figure out the deep meaning behind those strange lyrics. 'Don't Let Me Down'—wow, heavy, man! 'The Long and Winding Road'—sung on the bus as it wound through the Alps on my college art tour.

"Just name a song, and I'll give you a memory."

Chapter Nine: *The White Album*—
November 22, 1968

The White Album *was released five years to the day of the release of* **With The Beatles**, *their second album.*

I cross Commonwealth Avenue. It is a cool, late November day. Full of anticipation, I buy the new album and hurry home to my Beacon Street apartment. I peel back the plastic wrapper, gaze at the 8 x 10 photos of Paul and George and John and Ringo, gently drop the needle on the record, and take off with "Back in the USSR." The Beatles have done it again. I tack their pictures on the wall and listen to all four sides of the album, over and over, well into the night.

That Thanksgiving, I affect a Lennon look, adorned in wire rim glasses. The glasses are a prop, my means of getting close to Lennon. My eyesight is 20-20, though my mind is not!

Lennon's avant-garde lifestyle, where life was art, permeated this most expansive album The Beatles ever produced. The Beatles boasted an all-white cover, a Yoko Ono tape loop on one convoluted song, and a photo of Lennon, on the phone, in bed, nude. The Beatles produced a blockbuster, setting forth in several new directions of musical initiative simultaneously.

IT WAS 40 YEARS AGO TODAY

It was November 1968, and a new Beatles album had just been released. It proved the best-selling Beatles album of all time.

Paul McCartney provided the impetus to record this multitude of songs, many from a backlog of tunes composed in India earlier that year. McCartney can be credited with the drive to organize the music to create the album in the late summer of 1968. "Hey Jude"/"Revolution" was the single of the day, but The Beatles were already at work on another masterpiece.

The original title of this double album was *A Doll's House*. The name embossed on the pure white cover was The Beatles. Quickly, however, it became known simply as *The White Album*.

There are many ways to categorize or dissect *The White Album*. It was the best-selling Beatles album of all time and tenth best-selling album in the United States. It was the first album released by Apple Corps, The Beatles' new record company. It was the first time The Beatles recorded on eight-track, instead of four-track tapes. It was the first album to have a song composed by Ringo Starr. And it was the first Beatle album to have female vocals (Yoko Ono, Linda Eastman, and Pattie Harrison sang back-up on *Birthday*.)

Song placement on the album was closely examined. "Wild Honey Pie" is the fifth song from the front, and "Honey Pie" is the fifth song from the end. And not every song The Beatles wrote made the cut. There were so many songs that Lennon's "Jealous Guy" and Harrison's "Not Guilty" were not included because space became a problem, even with a double album. The White Album runs ninety minutes, nearly four times the length of *Something New* or *Beatles '65*. The album self-consciously refers to itself, as "Savoy Truffle" references "Ob-La-Di, Ob-La-Da" and "Glass Onion" comments piously on earlier Beatles songs.

Released on November 22, 1968, in the United Kingdom, and three days later in the States, *The White Album* continues to amaze and gratify the hardened Beatle fan, from the initial blast of white sound to the fade-out schmaltz at the end.

The White Album had its genesis during The Beatles transcendental meditation experience in Rishikesh, India, in the winter of 1968. While they were supposed to be meditating, The Beatles found the environment conducive to composing, and over the weeks created nearly forty songs. As they returned to England in the spring of 1968, disillusioned with the Maharishi, they realized they had a trove of material to sort through. They gathered at George Harrison's house that May and sifted through their repertoire. The album expanded over the summer, as recording got underway, and was completed with 34 songs, enough to fill a double album. Another Beatle first.

Production of *The White Album* presaged the eventual demise of the group. There was infighting through the summer. This was the first album The Beatles attempted since the death of their manager, Brian Epstein, who had been rigorous in controlling their inflated egos. Even George Martin, master producer, could not constrain the growing independence and disdain within the group.

The White Album is a conglomeration of varied musical talents and interests. Some critics demean *The White Album* for its length or lack of focus, but the public found a myriad of reasons to praise the recording. It was a concoction of a number of musical styles, each separate building block adding to the sum of the whole.

The basic conceit was to go back to basics, a reversion to The Beatles' roots in rock and roll, a '50s revival. Because The Beatles were so sophisticated, they satirized their idols and performed the style of song in many cases better than the original. This album stands alone in how The Beatles could mimic the very influences of their musical background.

To sample the menu proffered by *The White Album* is to view the individual strengths (and limitations) of The Beatles as musicians.

Their songs range from trite love songs to biting social commentary.

One could critique the number of songs by composer (John had 14, Paul 12, George 4 and Ringo 1), by minutes of music (John had 44.87, Paul had 27.03, George had 12.06 and Ringo 3.50), by collaboration between Lennon and McCartney (one: "Birthday"), but the most consistent manner is to start with the sound of the jet plane taking off in "Back in the USSR" and trace the album through to the sappy sounds of "Good Night." *The White Album* is a challenging journey, but well worth the ride.

Paul blasts off *The White Album* with "Back in the USSR." The sound of the jet shifts from one speaker to the other as The Beatles embark on their next big adventure.

While in India, Mike Love of the Beach Boys, suggested McCartney utilize the Beach Boys sound. McCartney latched onto "California Girls," snagged his title from Chuck Berry's "Back in the U.S.A." and parodied Ray Charles' "Georgia on My Mind," as The Beatles sang about all the pretty Russian girls in "Back in the USSR."

Urban legend claims The Beatles made an emergency landing in Moscow or actually performed a concert there. Not true. What is true is that the fierce drum playing in "Back in the USSR" was not performed by Ringo, but by Paul himself.

Ringo broke from The Beatles in a self-imposed exile, from August 22 to September 4, 1968 in an impetuous holiday to Sardinia to get away from the acrimony which roiled the group. It was two weeks before pleading by the rest of the band enticed him back, and welcomed his return with drums bedecked with flowers. Ringo's blatant act was a clear indication all was not well in the world of The Beatles.

"Dear Prudence," the second song on the album, is a pretty poem, the type John Lennon might have composed in art school to entice a girl he had his eye on. "Dear Prudence," of course, was written by Lennon for Mia Farrow's sister Prudence. He considered it one of his favorites.

In India, Prudence played a reclusive, hard-to-get ingénue, locking herself in her room to study, yet flattered by Lennon's attention. Although The Beatles left India early, Mia, Prudence, and others continued the course of study. Prudence later taught transcendental meditation and went on to teach elementary school.

With "Glass Onion" John Lennon teased fans with in-jokes about Beatle songs, as he peeled through layers of innuendo with oblique references to "Lady Madonna," "Strawberry Fields," "I Am the Walrus," "Fool on a Hill" and "Fixing a Hole." The line about Paul being the walrus was an attempt to show John and Paul were still close, although the symbol of the walrus may refer to death, which added to the "Paul is dead" legend.

Supposedly Paul was killed in an auto accident during the *Pepper* recordings, which gave rise to the "Paul is dead" myth. Clues surfaced in song and album sleeves as to his demise and replacement by a look-alike.

A glass onion is an English monocle, or single eyeglass. It also is a coffin with a transparent top, so mourners can get a last look at the departed. Lennon peeled back the many layers of his onion in song. With a heavy dose of satire, Lennon kept his audience awake, attuned to each nuance and pun. "Glass Onion" drew attention to Lennon's wry sense of humor.

Everyone sings along with "Ob-La-Di, Ob-La-Da," McCartney's tale of Desmond and Molly Jones falling in love, getting married, and raising their children in suburbia.

In Jamaican, the words "Ob-La-Di, Ob-La-Da" mean "life goes on," which is what the song is about. "Ob-La-Di, Ob-La-Da" has a reggae beat. It gave a nod to the number of Jamaicans in Great Britain. McCartney meant the song to be sung slowly, but after dozens of takes, Lennon sat down at the piano and hammered out the opening bars in a rousing honky-tonk beat, and the song took off.

The role reversal in the final verse, with Desmond putting on his face, was in error, supposedly, but McCartney didn't want to do another take. It is amusing to think of the ambiguities of a cross-dressing couple.

"Wild Honey Pie" is more a snippet than a song, lasting a mere 52 seconds. Paul McCartney wanted to experiment with multi-track tapes. He alone sang, played acoustic guitar and drums, building the song with multiple recordings. "Wild Honey Pie" evolved from a sing-along in India, although McCartney claimed it was a reference to "Honey Pie," elsewhere on the album.

For the listening audience, unaware of the background of Lennon's "The Continuing Story of Bungalow Bill," one considers it a metaphor on the United States involvement in Vietnam. It presents a blatant attack on America's foreign policy, filled with bravado and arrogance. Lennon flexed his anti-war muscles, and the public assumed that was the meat of the song. Lennon's anger at the senseless killing in Southeast Asia was evident. From his prominent opposition to the war in Vietnam he became a major figure in the peace movement, and earned the ire of the Nixon White House.

Lennon allegedly wrote "The Continuing Story of Bungalow Bill" in India about a wealthy young American who went tiger-hunting, then returned to the ashram to practice transcendental meditation with the Maharishi. Lennon belittled this spoiled American, modeled on Jungle Jim, a boyhood character. Yoko Ono sang a solo line and Maureen Starkey sang harmony in this song. It was the first time a female sang solo in a Beatles song. "The Continuing Story of Bungalow Bill" was recorded overnight on October 8, 1968, near the end of *The White Album* sessions.

Amid the internal disagreement in *The White Album*, George

Harrison felt shunted by Lennon and McCartney. The others did not appreciate" While My Guitar Gently Weeps," until Harrison brought in Eric Clapton to play lead. With Clapton, the band temporarily united, and the song was recorded as a masterful composition. The Beatles enjoyed working with Clapton, and when Harrison later threatened to leave because of the unrest, John Lennon considered Clapton to replace him. As it was, Clapton and Harrison ended up switching wives, but that's a tabloid tale for another day.

"While My Guitar Gently Weeps" stands as one of Harrison's premier songs. He was the master at evoking esoteric emotions of love, as he pleaded with people to pull together. The love that is asleep bespeaks the potential for world peace. We are slaves to the lives we lead and those who govern us. While the rhyme scheme was repetitive with diverted, perverted, inverted and alerted, this song remains one of Harrison's lasting ballads, a soft, sad look at the world.

George had been reading the I Ching about the relativism of facets of life, an eastern philosophy. The coincidence of events is the premise of western thought, which is a diametric opposing view. The I Ching noted the impact of chance. By chance, George opened a book at random, and his eye fell of the words "gently weeps." The song was born.

An unused verse in "While My Guitar Gently Weeps" refers to a helpless bystander who observes the troubles of the world that continue to rage. Harrison feels helpless, watching and worrying about the world. He's gradually aging but doing nothing while his guitar gently weeps.

George Martin handed Lennon a magazine article entitled, "Happiness is a warm gun in your hand." Lennon found the topic insane and distasteful. But then he sat down and wrote the song. From a musical perspective, "Happiness is a Warm Gun" is a mishmash of meters, speeding up and slowing down. It unites two songs, as the beat slows. Both Lennon and McCartney, though, considered it one of their favorites on *The White Album*.

Allusions to heroin, sexual fantasies, or shooting someone (a warm gun has just been shot) make the song as controversial as anything Lennon wrote. That the National Rifle Association co-opted the slogan "Happiness is a warm gun" from the *Peanuts* cartoon by Charles Schulz, "Happiness is a warm puppy," adds to the multiple takes on the song.

(Of course, "Happiness is a Warm Gun" makes the unintended tragic prediction of Lennon's murder by gunshots in 1980, at the hand of Mark David Chapman.)

On the flip side of the first disc, McCartney shares his emotions toward his sheepdog, "Martha," in a saucy, sappy tune, based loosely on a 19th century Viennese opera. McCartney claims the song is a tribute to his muse, the source of inspiration for his musical compositions. At the time he wrote the song he was breaking up with Jane Asher. The simplest theme remains: a tribute to his sheepdog Martha.

McCartney's style is reminiscent of a piano played in a large music hall, with a brass band accompaniment. McCartney and George Martin were the primary players in the production of this song.

Lennon was an insomniac. After three weeks of intense meditation and missing Yoko Ono, he composed "I'm So Tired" and recorded it at three o'clock in the morning. It evokes a lost and lonely time, with little sense of hope.

"I'm So Tired" delved into a drugged-out experience. It can be interpreted as an effort to clear his mind from dependence on barbiturates, alcohol, and tobacco. He appeared worn down by life, depressed, and the song was an effort to regain control and recapture his strength.

In passing, "I'm So Tired" referred to the harmful effects of smoking. Sir Walter Raleigh imported tobacco to England from Virginia. That was stupid, says Lennon.

At the end, Lennon mutters "Monsieur, monsieur, monsieur, how about another one." When "Paul is dead" fanatics played this backwards, it sounded like, "Paul is dead; miss him, miss him, miss him."

In the spring of 1968, following the assassination of Reverend Martin Luther King, race riots spread through cities across the United States. McCartney, holed up in his Scotland sheep farm, wrote "Blackbird" as a tribute to the civil rights struggle by black Americans. It is a moving melody, with a hopefulness that still awaits actualization on both sides of the Atlantic. "Blackbird" is an example of the pronounced awareness of political overtones in Beatle songs.

The crowing of blackbirds was dubbed in later. McCartney lifted the riff from a Bach classical guitar piece he and Harrison had played in their youth. McCartney was alone in the recording studio for this song, and his tapping foot can be heard.

In the summer of 1968, with a police riot at the Democratic convention in Chicago, protestors cursed police with the epithet of pigs. It was assumed "Piggies" targeted police.

George Harrison garnered four songs on *The White Album*, one on each side. "Piggies" was intended as an attack on corporate greed, akin to "Taxman," with an anti-establishment take. With a nod to George Orwell's *Animal Farm* and William Golding's *Lord of the Flies*, Harrison sang about pigs who rule.

One verse was omitted from *The White Album*. It mentions the pranks the piggies play, with reference to piggy banks, and even pays homage to Pig Brother. Harrison was nearly as deft at Lennon with his puns.

The song includes a harpsichord and a string quartet, and the oinks of hungry pigs, added by Lennon for effect. The Beatles became vegetarians during their Indian sojourn, so the last line was a tinge ironic. *Piggies* is part of a trilogy of animal songs, squeezed into the second side of *The White Album*.

McCartney wrote "Rocky Raccoon" in India, and played it for songsmith Donovan Leitch. It is a parody of Bob Dylan's nasal voice and his country album *Nashville Skyline*. In recording *The White Album*, George Martin played a honky-tonk piano, and John Lennon picked up the harmonica. The story recounts the adventures of a cowboy, Rocky, who tries to kill the man who stole his woman. In the attack, Rocky is wounded, and crawls back to his hotel room, where he stumbles over Gideon's Bible.

In 1966, John Lennon's remark that The Beatles were more popular than Jesus caused a major upset in the Bible belt of the United States. The Christian right was outraged, and launched an attack on The Beatles, burning records and haranguing them on radio. McCartney was hurt by the damage to the public image of The Beatles, and it is posited he wrote "Rocky Raccoon" to repel attacks on Lennon's remark and put the story to rest.

If one considered The Beatles as Rocky, they stole the hearts of young Christians. Evangelicals sought revenge. Rocky, as The Beatles, was wounded by Lennon's remark on Christianity. Yet The Beatles survive when they crawl back to Britain.

Two references to Gideon appear in the song. The Gideon Bible group places Bibles in hotel rooms. During The Beatles final tour, apparently the Gideons attempted to put Bibles on Beatle plane seats. "Rocky Raccoon" is a rollicking country song, regardless of its religiosity take.

Ringo Starr began to write a song in 1963, but didn't finish it until The Beatles journeyed to India, five years later. By finally composing a song, Ringo implied he wanted to be taken seriously, both in love and song. In this simple, pleading love song, "Don't

Pass Me By," the persona awaits his lover, fearing she's left him for another.

"Don't Pass Me By" was recorded in the early summer of 1968. The first take was titled "Ringo's Tune," the second was "Some Kind of Friendly." It debuted as "Don't Pass Me By" on June 12, 1968 and proved to be a number-one hit in Sweden.

McCartney sought to show he could still belt it out, as he had so long ago with his rendition of "Long Tall Sally." Since *The White Album* was a return to roots, McCartney chose that route to epitomize his capacity as a rock singer.

"Why Don't We Do It in the Road" is a pounding, blasting jam session, a loud, short blast of repetitive rock and roll, basically raucous screaming by Paul, with Ringo keeping time, clapping his hands. The simple lyrics were inspired in India, when Paul saw a group of monkeys on the street. One monkey hopped on another, consummated the act, then continued on his way. Paul appreciated the simplicity of procreation, and the song came to life.

Paul and Ringo closeted themselves to record the song; John was upset not to be included in recording "Why Don't We Do It in the Road," which came near the end of the *White Album* recording sessions, as tensions had exacerbated.

From the loud, hard, fast, short "Why Don't We Do It in the Road," McCartney shifted gears dramatically with a touching love song, "I Will," dedicated to his future wife Linda Eastman. Written in India, the song bespeaks his romantic feelings, as if he's always loved her, and always will. It is a plaintive piece, begging for love, and promising to wait for her forever. They were married in March 1969, and enjoyed nearly three decades of matrimony before she succumbed to breast cancer in 1998.

This romantic ode of eternal love is expressive of McCartney's optimistic attitude, ripe with commercial appeal. Some say it was just a silly love song, too bland to carry a message, but it fit the tenor of the times and proved true to McCartney's heart.

"I Will" was covered by Ben Taylor, son of James Taylor and Carly Simon, in the 1995 movie *Bye Bye Love*, starring Paul Reiser. James Taylor got his big break as one of the young artists brought into Apple Corps as an intern with The Beatles.

"I Will" melds seamlessly into Lennon's "Julia," a poignant tribute to his mother.

Lennon's contributions to *The White Album* reflected the rapid changes in his personal life in 1968. His mother was named Julia, hence the title of the tune. An inebriated off-duty policeman killed her, when Lennon was 18. John's son Julian was named for his mother.

In a complicated metaphor, Lennon compared his mother's virtues to those of his lover, Yoko Ono as "Julia" became an ode to his newfound love. Yoko means "ocean child" in Japanese, and references to the sea permeate the song. The opening lines were lifted from the poet Kahil Gibran.

While McCartney recorded a number of songs by himself for *The White Album*, "Julia" was the only song Lennon wrote and recorded by himself, with an acoustic guitar. He had learned a new fingerpicking technique in India from Donovan, and this was his inaugural effort.

Side three of *The White Album* opens with a joyful, catchy jam entitled "Birthday," the only collaboration between John and Paul on *The White Album*. Waiting for a rehearsal to begin, they just rolled into it. Admittedly it's a take-off on "Happy Birthday," as The Beatles just break into this loud, fast, happy song. Paul played a piano hooked up like a harpsichord for special effects. Yoko Ono and Pattie Harrison sang back up. In this cheery tune, you can almost see the smiles that carry the song along.

(During the recording of George Harrison's "All Things Must

Pass" in 1970, the band burst into a spontaneous tribute to John Lennon with, "It's Johnny's Birthday." Lennon was about to turn thirty.)

In "Birthday" McCartney delivered a satiric jab at the cha-cha generation of the Chuck Berry era, urging his listeners in a playful riff to take a "cha-cha-cha chance." His uncanny knack for mimicry populated *The White Album*.

"Yer Blues" is a more somber song. While it's a parody of British blues, it allowed John Lennon a little self-analysis. He makes reference to the suicide in Dylan's "Ballad of a Thin Man." Part of the song was recorded before Lennon finished the lyrics, so one verse has indistinguishable vocals. The style is basic, without electronic fanfare or studio touch-ups. Ringo claimed this recording was one of his favorites, as The Beatles were secluded in a large closet at the Abbey Road studio, and just let the music out in a tight embrace.

In 1969 Lennon performed "Yer Blues" at the Toronto Rock 'n' Roll Revival, the only Beatles song he sang. He later performed "Yer Blues" for a televised performance of the Rolling Stones Rock 'n' Roll Circus, accompanied by Eric Clapton, Keith Richards, and Mitch Mitchell, though the program was never aired. (In 1995 it was released as a video.)

In stark contrast to "Yer Blues," McCartney wrote "Mother Nature's Son" after listening to a lecture on nature by the Maharishi Mahesh Yogi in India. It's easily hummed, with simplistic lyrics. The carefree sense of the outdoors is evident, as the persona, appreciates the environment around us. This is a Beatles "green" song.

"Mother Nature's Son" was influenced by the ethereal music of Donovan, with his gentle, out-of-doors images. John Denver was going to use the title for his *Rocky Mountain High* album. Instead, it titled a biography of the singer, following his untimely death.

"Everybody's Got Something to Hide Except Me and My

Monkey." The title is longer than the song. This was a chance for Lennon to let his ya-yas out and express his devotion to Yoko. He felt people around them were paranoid, and he and Yoko were the only sane ones. "Everybody's Got Something to Hide" is long, loud, and hard. True Lennon! The lines of screeching, even belligerent music exemplified a charged-up Lennon in his pursuit to resurrect and recapture basic rock and roll.

McCartney's "Why Don't We Do It in the Road" focused on copulating monkeys, while Lennon's "Everybody's Got Something to Hide Except Me and My Monkey" kept the monkey off their backs.

Lennon cast his complaint about the Maharishi in song. "Sexie Sadie" was an admission The Beatles felt hoodwinked by the Maharishi's allusion to revealing the essence or answer to the meaning of life. Lennon thought the Maharishi had let them down, physically by flirting with the women and spiritually by not delivering essential elements they sought. "Sexie Sadie" obscured the Maharishi in a thinly veiled metaphor, and like many Beatle songs, expressed an opinion couched in convoluted lyrics.

Lennon skewered a man he once adored. The Maharishi proved a mercenary with an exploitive nature, all too human, which Lennon found disillusioning. He came to realize the Maharishi was just another money-grubber, clothed in the rags of the lord. The Beatles had misread him, though he had offered spiritual guidance following the death of Epstein.

Paul McCartney wrote "Helter Skelter" in response to complaints he only wrote ballads. "Helter Skelter" is no ballad. Its raw, raucous sound presaged heavy-metal rock. Its vintage rock, loud, crude, and rough, was propelled by a throbbing beat. The pleading, piercing sounds are uttered in a quest for recognition. The ragged edges of the song demand attention and add to the impromptu tension, an urgency and vibrancy that envelopes and overwhelms the listener.

McCartney wanted to write the loudest rock song he could, in response to Pete Townsend of The Who, who set the bar with "I Can See for Miles." "Helter Skelter" is the name of an amusement park ride in Britain, and McCartney drew a metaphor between the ride from the bottom to the top and the rise and fall of the Roman and British Empires. All things come and go, ebb and flow. ("Helter Skelter is referenced in Don McLean's *American Pie*, an ode to rock music of the sixties.")

An early version of the song lasted 27 minutes, but the final cut is a mere four-and-a-half minutes. Like "Rain," "Strawberry Fields Forever," and "Hello Goodbye," "Helter Skelter" fades out then returns to repeat with another ending. The eerie repetition brings the song back into focus again, so we feel a sense of déjà vu: we've been here before.

"Helter Skelter" finally came to an end with the infamous complaint by Ringo Starr, as he tossed his drumsticks across the room: "I got blisters on my fingers!" Ringo recalled the studio atmosphere as total madness. In one incident, George Harrison dashed across the room, a flaming ashtray in hand.

Charles Manson used "Helter Skelter" as an excuse for his 1969 California murders. He believed The Beatles predicted a race war with "Helter Skelter", "Piggies" and "Blackbird," and he, Manson, was responsible to start the war between blacks and whites. He claimed his ultimate calling was to rule the world. For ordering the Tate-Labianca murders, he is spending his life in prison.

It is a relief when "Helter Skelter" finally fades out, then slams shut. George Harrison picks up the pieces with a love song, ambiguously addressed to his lover or his lord, entitled "Long, Long, Long." The sweet cadence of calming words evokes a peacefulness that drapes the listener after the rancorous crashing sounds of "Helter Skelter." Harrison claimed the song was written for God, but it could as easily refer to his woman. His calm follows the storm.

The Beatles recorded "Long, Long, Long" 67 times, before it met their stringent standards. At the end of the song an unusual sound arises. A bottle of Blue Nun, balanced on a speaker, started to wobble and rattle as McCartney played the organ. This tidbit of Beatle musicology added to the mystique of *The White Album*.

Lennon challenged listeners with "Revolution 1," which kicks off the fourth and final side of *The White Album*. He wrote this in response to the Rolling Stones' "Street Fighting Man" and in support of French student uprisings in the politically charged spring of 1968.

"Revolution 1" was recorded six weeks prior to the faster version, which landed on the flip side of "Hey Jude." This original version, "Revolution 1," slower, with a more measured beat, has a distinct difference in the lyrics. When Lennon sang about destruction, he said you can count him out, then added "in," to create ambiguity in his message. He was aware of the youth movement and wanted to play both sides, but challenged his audience to see what was going on.

McCartney reached back to the music hall era with "Honey Pie," including a scratchy old 78-rpm record to lend the feel of early 20th century music, adding brass and woodwind backup to authenticate the sound. "Honey Pie" could be an extension of "Lovely Rita," from the *Sgt. Pepper* era. The singer pleads with his girl to come home, but she's a hit in Hollywood. He's too lazy to follow, yet fears he'll lose her. The song is a tease, a light and lively take on boy meets girl.

"Savoy Truffle" was a paean to Harrison's good friend Eric Clapton, a master guitarist. The lyrics for "Savoy Truffle" were plucked from the lid of a box of Mackintosh Good News chocolates, and the song sticks together well. The probability of cavities from too many sweets was mentioned when Harrison warned of the need to have one's teeth pulled out. The assorted chocolate flavors worked into the song include Coffee Dessert, Ginger Sling, Cream Tangerine and Montelimart. This amusing tribute immortalized Clapton for his chocolate addiction. It was said he could devour a box of chocolates at a single sitting.

Lennon's "Cry Baby Cry" is a good-natured tease, poking fun at the pomp and pageantry of British royalty. "Cry Baby Cry" slyly pulled back the curtain of the imagined tribulations of royalty, with a tale told in child-like innocence. "Cry Baby Cry" features a beautiful melody, but the story is spurious.

"Cry Baby Cry" was based on an advertisement that read, "Cry baby cry, make your mother buy." The song originated as a fairy tale from Lennon's youth, about the lords and ladies putting on a séance for the children. Lennon characterized the duke and duchess as buffoons, with him worrying about a speech for the Bird and Bee, while she arrives late for tea. Horrors! The Duchess of Kirkcaldy was an imaginary person, but The Beatles did play in Kirkcaldy back in 1963.

At the end of "Cry Baby Cry," we sense another song, which doesn't develop. "Can You Take Me Back" is a McCartney tune, followed by a conversation recorded between George Martin and assistant Alistair Taylor over the latter forgetting to bring a bottle of claret to the studio. The tiniest incident was fodder for The Beatles. The conversation segues into "Revolution 9."

"Revolution 9" started as a coda for "Revolution 1," with the words "all right," but Lennon added multiple sound clips and tape loops, with fading and repetition, to create a most unusual piece. At eight minutes, thirteen seconds," Revolution 9" is the longest track The Beatles ever recorded and took the most time to create. No doubt Lennon enjoyed authorship of "Revolution 9," and with

Yoko's assistance, it can be considered a work of art, though not a typical Beatles tune.

The repetition of "number nine," lifted from an EMI test tape, persists through the song, fading in and returning when least expected. This motif adds a semblance of continuity to the chaotic sounds and exclamations, squeaks and whistles, which appear and disappear at whim. It's a long, strange experience.

"Revolution 9" is a collage of sounds, a series of tapes that wind and rewind, loop over and repeat through one another, an audio stream of consciousness. It opens with John and Yoko awakening in bed. Orchestral tuning, a tad of Beethoven, and even a bit from *Pepper* are audible. Someone practicing the recorder keeps returning, trying to get the notes right. Harrison and Lennon converse obtusely amid cheers at a football game. The words "all right" are heard, left over from "Revolution 1," as well as a snippet from Harrison's "While My Guitar Gently Weeps." A baby whimpers, sirens, gun shots, and the tortured sound "hub-buba-buba" is heard. As this "number nine" test tape resurfaces, we hear the final admonition: "Take this, brother; may it serve you well." With subtler, juxtaposed sounds, "Revolution 9" draws to a close after more than eight minutes, an intriguing experiment, and a long, long way from "She Loves You."

Paul McCartney and George Martin were adamantly opposed to inclusion of the song on *The White Album*. They felt the influence of Yoko Ono was detrimental to the overall impression of the album, and "Revolution 9" was too much. As an artist in her own right, Yoko Ono presented an avant-garde approach to John Lennon, and he incorporated her style in his music.

With "I Am the Walrus," Lennon introduced a tad of nonsense verse and recorded radio play. Rumor has it that there is an intriguing, unreleased recording entitled "Carnival of Light," by McCartney, created during the *Pepper* session. This, too, is an avant-garde effort, more than a dozen minutes long, and more than forty years old.

One more tidbit is that Charles Manson thought "Revolution 9" was an interpretation of the biblical book Revelation, chapter 9, which deals with the apocalypse. Manson used "Revolution 9" as further justification to initiate race warfare.

"Revolution 9" eventually fades into "Good Night," as *The White Album* slides into its final number. "Good Night" was sung by Ringo accompanied by a thirty-piece orchestra, conducted by George Martin. "Good Night" was a lullaby Lennon composed for Julian, then five years old. (Julian didn't learn of the origins of the song until his father's death in 1980, when he was also told that he was the inspiration for "Hey Jude.")

"Good Night" fits into the genre of satire, one of a mélange of songs layered with spoof and excess that flows throughout the double discs. It was intentionally overly orchestrated, previewing Phil Spector's "wall of sound," yet it exudes a smooth richness, a fitting close for the album.

The song is schmaltzy and extravagant. Lennon's goal was to make it an over-the-top production. As a parody of big-band music, the song works. As a closing number for the eponymous *White Album*, it works. As representative of the wild and varied talents of The Beatles, it fits. But as a song for the ages, it verges on mediocrity. Lennon, in the voice of Ringo, wishes us each a good night as he concludes the album with a dose of grandeur.

* * *

While their individual strengths had matured, The Beatles lost much of their cohesion, and *The White Album* proved more a collection of random musical fantasies of four young men than the product of a tight rock band. *The White Album* is a challenge to get one's ears around and summarize, but certainly a treat to experience with its sprawling musical array.

The White Album is long. Thirty songs take over an hour and a half to listen to, and the style is disjointed. Yet that was the intent. The Beatles were not creating a rock opera or a collection of greatest hits. They sought to show themselves where they were at that particular point in time.

The White Album was an amalgam of basic rock. Lennon's songs characterize that intent. The Beatles used *The White Album* as a means to honor their musical heritage, both personally and politically. They parodied the competition: that was McCartney's forte. *The White Album* is laden with style and substance. What it lacks in thematic cohesion, it makes up in variety. With *The White Album*, The Beatles cleaned out the backlog of songs composed during their sojourn to India in early 1968.

Paul McCartney spearheaded the production of *The White Album*, as he had *Pepper* and *Mystery Tour*. Without his commercial savvy and competent musician skills, the album would not have succeeded. It was a challenge to rein in the varied approaches of The Beatles at the time, and it was well done.

Time magazine reviewed the album on December 12, 1968 and wrote that the album encompassed a wide autobiographic anthology of The Beatles varied abilities: "Skill and sophistication abound, but so does a faltering sense of taste and purpose. The album's thirty tracks are a sprawling motley assemblage of The Beatles' best abilities and worst tendencies…. But when the foursome meander from style to style without any apparent guiding objective or sense of urgency, they seem to be substituting synthetics for synthesis."

If *Rubber Soul* represents The Beatles in their Baroque style, and *Sgt. Pepper* is their Classic effort, then *The Beatles*, or their *White Album*, becomes their Mannerist phase, very good, but more diffuse than previous efforts. *The White Album* is where The Beatles were in the autumn of 1968, free from the pressures of touring, limited only by their creative abilities and genius. It was time to "Get Back" and "Let It Be."

* * *

Glenna Barkan (retired) recalls she bought a copy of *The White Album* for her two daughters. To share. *"Boy, that was a mistake,"* she says. *"I was so foolish to think they would share."* Even though *The White Album* had two records, it wasn't enough. Each daughter needed her own album.

On holding a celebration for the anniversary of the *Sgt. Pepper* album, **Carl Mueller (potter) says**: *"Why not do* **The White Album***? I had the earlier ones, like* **Rubber Soul***, but what makes* **Pepper** *so special?"*

John Zielin: (techie): *"I remember buying* **The White Album** *the day it came out. There was a little record shop; it was underground, across from BU. And I had heard the album was coming out, and I was one of the first to buy it that day. That's what stays in my memory."*

Judy Case (therapeutic recreation director): *"I saw the absolute best Beatles tribute ever, at 7 Angels Theatre in Waterbury, Connecticut, this past April (saw it 4x actually!) It was called 'Yesterday & Today' and starred Billy McGuigan. He and his 2 brothers, and 4 backup musicians, did a show where the audience picked their favorite Beatles song and told why, so the show was different each time. They knew them all, and sounded* **so** *much like the real thing, especially the instrumentals, every detail! (They weren't trying to look or each one 'be' a Beatle). I've seen Beatlemania twice, and lots of cover bands, but none this good. I wish they'd do it again!"*

Chapter Ten: *Let It Be* (recorded January 1969)—Released May 8, 1970

In the spring of 1969, months before graduation, I have to face my future. I had discussed with my parents, friends, and peers that there was no way I would serve in Vietnam. I'd go to Canada instead. I was absolutely serious.

I request a hearing with my draft board, in Spencer, Massachusetts, in March. I sit at a rickety card table with three big men in suits and discuss my determination not to fight. I have documents and reference letters on my commitment. I am very nervous, but the preparation pays off, and I am granted a conscientious objector deferment. When it comes time for my physical, and the option of alternative service, I fail the exam and am classified 4-F.

In the autumn of 1969 there is a moratorium to end the war. I march down Commonwealth Avenue with thousands of people, thousands of cheering, chanting people, singing Lennon's anthem, "Give Peace a Chance." That memorable moment, seeing the crowds gathered in the streets, lives with me. Yet the war drags on another six years.

Again, in 2004, I march through New York City with my daughter Jill, chanting Lennon's familiar refrain, in protest against another senseless, endless war.

Flush from the success of their first double album, The Beatles quickly regrouped in the recording studio in early 1969, intent on capitalizing on their resurgent success and eager to return to their rock-and-roll roots. *The White Album* exemplified their musical range and ability; now they felt the time was ripe to explore their inner workings, the behind-the-scenes ambiance of the recording studio, the creativity and mechanics of song writing, recording, and production.

Once again Paul McCartney took the lead. He conceived the idea to tape the wit and wisdom of The Beatles at work and play, then produce it, as it were, without editing. From that rough concept, he wanted to videotape The Beatles in action, culminating in a grand television spectacular, perhaps even a live concert following the studio sessions. Such a concert would be a major event in itself, at a Roman amphitheater in North Africa or aboard a cruise ship in the Mediterranean, telecast around the world.

The concept of a made-for-TV movie about The Beatles, as they created an album, was unique. The album would incorporate conversational tidbits to supplement the songs. There would be old chestnuts, familiar favorites, and, of course, new Beatle songs. The basic intent was to expand on the theme of *The White Album* and explore the depths of their rock origins.

Get Back/Let It Be never became the album or film it was intended. Recorded in January 1969, shortly after the release of *The White Album*, it took more than a year to resolve the disagreements and salve the bruised egos that arose during the recording and filming sessions. The tapes were shelved as The Beatles sorted out their various business ventures, personal angst, and musical preferences on the recordings.

The album *Let It Be* was finally released on May 8, 1970, nearly a year and a half after the recording sessions. Their final album, it proved a coda to The Beatles' career, their swan song; a request to let it be.

IT WAS 40 YEARS AGO TODAY

* * *

(Because the **Get Back/Let It Be** *recording sessions occurred prior to Abbey Road, their final musical production, we cover those songs now.)*

The *Get Back/Let It Be* sessions began a mere ten weeks after The Beatles wrapped *The White Album*, and lasted through a tumultuous month of January 1969. These sessions, at Twickenham Studios at 3 Saville Row, London, exacerbated the discord and rancor of the five month recording sessions for *The White Album*, which, in turn, acknowledged disparity and disharmony within the group. *Get Back* was an effort to bring The Beatles back together, but the dissonant personalities led to an untenable situation. The internal crises were apparent in the disparate nature of the album, and glaringly evident in the film version of *Let It Be*.

Lennon's famous line, "I hope we pass the audition," set the tone for the album, which offered an intimate, and ultimately unflattering portrait of The Beatles' recording techniques and styles. Hundreds of hours of tapes caught them in a time warp, recording covers of old favorites, dabbling with a few new songs, and, intriguingly, offering preliminary versions of their final cuts, to emerge later in 1969, under the eponymous title, *Abbey Road*.

It is evident, from the vantage of hindsight, that significant disagreements were at play. John, George, and Ringo resented Paul's discipline and direction. From the film of the sessions it was clear that Paul dominated and controlled the others.

John was withdrawn from the group, but attentive to his beloved Yoko, who often spoke for him. They were into heroin and each other. George grew resentful, feeling a lack of respect from both John and Paul. On January 10, 1969, a week into rehearsals, George stormed out of the studio in a rage, announcing he was "leaving the band for now." He did return within days, but this was the second

Beatle to express, by his actions, that the fractured attitudes were destroying the foundation of the group.

The show went on. On January 22 George brought in Billy Preston, and his appearance brightened the other Beatles, and their work showed marked improvement. This action mirrored Harrison's introduction of Eric Clapton during *The White Album* sessions.

As if to dispel the disharmony, John and Paul sang "Two of Us" as if they were school chums back in Liverpool. Paul ostensibly wrote "Two of Us" about his girlfriend Linda Eastman, yet the lyrics speak affectionately to John, and the camaraderie the two composers shared over the years. There's a sense of nostalgia, heading home, with memories longer than their future. How true. On the album John and Paul sing the song together, a harmonious, acoustic piece that resonates through the years.

In "Dig a Pony," John included a reference to the group's earlier incarnation as Johnny and the Moondogs, the name The Beatles sang under when they appeared in a talent show in 1960. John wrote the song for his beloved Yoko, and perhaps in her honor, Lennon reveled in a litany of mismatched phrases and confusing lyrics.

(As the recording of "Dig a Pony" got underway in the rooftop concert, Ringo started to sneeze and mopped his brow. This intimate inclusion offered an immediacy and charm to the film.)

The words for "Across the Universe" came to Lennon while he was married to Cynthia, and she was talking at him. He felt her words swirling around in his mind, and the song came to life. Unable to sleep that night, he got up and wrote down the lyrics. It is one of his more memorable tunes, with words supplemented by bird sounds and an ethereal affection for natural images. Abstract scenes float through the song, like the sounds of birds in flight. "Across the Universe" was a favorite of Lennon's. He considered it his most poetic lyric. (And across the universe was a film that gloried in The Beatles' music, released in 2007.)

When Phil Spector completed his "Wall of Sound" dramatization, the song assumed a more ponderous tone, with the words slogging heavily across the sky instead of flitting lightly here and there (In the stripped down, "original" *Let It Be...Naked* album, released in 2003, flocks of birds flap their wings at the onset and closing of the song.

"Across the Universe" includes the meditative phrase "om," considered the primary vibration/cosmic sound of the universe. Transcendental meditation permeates the song. And the Sanskrit words "Jai Guru Deva Un offer a mantra of thanks to Guru Dev, victory to the divine god, the wise man who taught the Maharishi.

Initially, "Across the Universe" was to be the B side to "Lady Madonna," but Harrison's "Inner Light" preempted that coveted spot. In late 1968, just prior to the *Get Back* sessions, "Across the Universe" was previewed at a charity event.

(Sean Lennon performed "Across the Universe," in 2001 at the John Lennon tribute in Madison Square Garden. What a moving experience for the son to emulate his father in song! After the Asian tsunami in 2005 Brian Wilson, Bono, Tim McGraw, Stevie Wonder, Norah Jones, and Alecia Keys headlined a group that sang it at the Grammies to raise monies for the victims. This version of "Across the Universe" was the fastest selling download on iTunes and charted at #22 on the Billboard top 100.)

(And on February 4, 2008, "Across the Universe" was the first track beamed into outer space by NASA in honor of its fiftieth anniversary and the song's fortieth. "Across the Universe" was aimed at the North Star, some 431 light-years away.)

"I Me Mine" speaks to the Hindu term for the ego, and is an effort to renounce selfish tendencies and thus unite with the lord. It is George Harrison's effort to find inner peace, although the song may well address internal conflicts among The Beatles as well. John Lennon did not participate in the recording of this song either time it was recorded.

Either time? It was first recorded early in 1969 in the *Get Back* sessions. George, Paul, and Ringo performed. John was present but dancing a waltz with Yoko, as seen in the film. A year later, January 3 and 4, 1970, George, Paul, and Ringo returned to the studio to re-record *I Me Mine* for the impending album. John had quit the group in September 1969, so again he was absent. George made an obtuse reference to Lennon's absence, but says confidently the others will carry on, and "good work will continue at number two," Abbey Road Studio Two.

The Beatles engaged Phil Spector to doctor up the tapes, and this song received the full Spector treatment, especially the over-dubbed string accompaniment. The song was so short, however, that Spector copied a section, and repeated it, to lengthen the tune. Allen Klein employed Spector against, or without, McCartney's wishes. (This song was stripped down to its basic elements in *Let It Be...Naked.*)

(*I Me Mine* was the title of George Harrison's 1980 limited-edition autobiography, reissued by Simon and Schuster in 2002 by Olivia Harrison.)

Like the wordless tune "Flying" from *Magical Mystery Tour,* "Dig It" was credited to all four Beatles. The 51-second clip on the *Let It Be* album was lifted from a twelve-minute jam that evolved from The Beatles singing an extended version of "Twist and Shout," with Billy Preston on the organ. Lennon introduced the song for the television version, which was never completed. He mentioned Georgie Wood, a music-hall performer, who stood less than five feet tall. Lennon then called off the songs The Beatles included in *Let It Be.*

The phrase, "dig it," was popular with The Beatles at the time.

("Dig It" itself was omitted from *Let It Be...Naked* and replaced with 'Don't Let Me Down.")

In the midst of the turmoil of the *Get Back/Let It Be* sessions, Paul McCartney was anxious and distraught. In a dream his late mother appeared to him, and said everything would be all right. He should just let it be. She had died of breast cancer when Paul was fourteen. McCartney felt blessed to receive this supernatural calming message of comfort.

On "Let it Be," Paul sang lead and played piano, with John and George in harmony. Linda Eastman sang back-up vocals. Billy Preston played the organ. "Let it Be" was a prominent part of the rooftop concert on January 30, 1969. George overdubbed the guitar the following January, so various versions of the song are out there.

("Let It Be" was the first Beatle single to make it to the Soviet Union, in 1972. Paul performed the song for Vladimir Putin at the Kremlin before he sang in a concert at Red Square. Paul, George, and Ringo sang it at Linda McCartney's funeral in 1998 at St. Martin in the Fields in Trafalgar Square. And Paul sang it for the Concert for New York following the World Trade Center attack in 2001. *Sesame Street* parodied the song as "Letter B.")

Lennon disapproved of the Christian influence of Mother Mary in "Let it Be" and requested "Maggie Mae" follow in the lineup. "Maggie Mae" is a song about prostitutes, a Liverpool tune, covered by numerous groups. The Beatles used to sing it as a warm-up to their act, and John Lennon played it at the church fair when he first met Paul McCartney, back in 1956. The point of the *Get Back* sessions was to revisit The Beatles' early music, so this was an appropriate choice.

For the first time since the *Help!* album, The Beatles recorded a song they didn't write. "Maggie Mae" was produced with a different spelling, perhaps for copyright purposes. It is the next to the shortest song The Beatles ever recorded, at a mere 40 seconds. (Like

"Dig It," "Maggie Mae" was omitted from the 2003 *Let It Be...Naked* album.)

The second side of the official *Let It Be* album kicks off with "I've Got a Feeling," the last song John and Paul actually composed together. Even that was unique. They worked two songs together, Paul's bubbly ode to Linda Eastman and John's despondent dirge of self-pity, "Everybody Had a Hard Year." While Paul wrote an uplifting love song, John spelled out a depressing litany, with each line starting with "Everybody." The two tunes were linked by Lennon's bridge from a third unfinished song, "Watching Rainbows." This song was sung with gusto in the rooftop concert, and featured in the film.

In stark chronological contrast to "I've Got a Feeling," "One After 909" was among the first Lennon-McCartney tunes, composed around 1958, a good decade earlier. The Beatles originally recorded it in 1963, but were unhappy with the results and shelved it. Since the *Get Back/Let It Be* sessions focused on a return to their roots, they recorded this version of "One After 909" with a heavier, faster beat, dominated by Harrison's guitar riffs.

The rocker tells the story of a girl who leaves her lover and heads off by train. She plans to board the "one after 909." He follows her, only to realize she was not on that train car. He returns home, discouraged, disoriented, and walks into the wrong house. For eighteen-year-old Lennon, it was a complex tale to put to music.

"Long and Winding Road" endured a tortured trek on its route to become the twenty-first (and final) number-one single by The Beatles, reaching that prized pinnacle on June 13, 1970, a month after its release.

The McCartney ballad was intended as an acoustic take on The Beatles themselves. Written in the height of discord in the autumn of 1968 amid *The White Album* sessions, the song describes the difficulties of a trail with no end, a challenge along the way. It's a melancholy take on unrequited love, but makes obvious comparisons to The Beatles themselves.

The song was said to be inspired by a drive along a thirty-mile route in Scotland, the B842, which runs near McCartney's sheep farm. It must be one of those roads that seems to go on forever, without an end. McCartney composed the song in Scotland, though it was ripe with the tension of The Beatles back in London.

George Harrison's :For You Blue" follows "Let It Be" on the album; both songs were on a single released from the album. Harrison penned this tune for his lover/wife, Pattie Boyd. When The Beatles recorded the song in January 1969, the working title was "George's Blues (Because You're Sweet and Lovely)". The title was revised in various incarnations of the album.

During the song, John plays a lap steel-slide guitar, and in the background George is heard to say, "Go, Johnny Go." Conversation tidbits that filtered into the album were intended to give a rough-hewn flavor to the experience of the music.

(In November 2002, Paul sang "For You Blue" at the memorial Concert for George on the anniversary of George Harrison's death.)

The original *Let It Be* album ended with the song that was intended as its title. "Get Back" has a catchy beat, and a vibrant playfulness that encourages a sing-along. It was supposed to exemplify The Beatles in their search for their roots, basic rock-and-roll elements. Instead, it offers a flight of imagination, a variation to "Rocky Raccoon," with a western flavor and a risqué storyline.

"Get Back" was an exercise in what The Beatles initially intended: the song was written in the studio as cameras and tape decks spun. That was the goal of the *Let It Be* sessions, and the last song on the album captures that essence.

Lennon said "Get Back" felt like an extension of "Lady Madonna," but there was more to it. Intended as a tribute to Linda

Eastman, Paul's lover, it references Tuscon, Arizona, where Linda lived and JoJo's, a popular bar, as well as her first husband, Joe See.

McCartney lifted a line from Harrison's "Sour Milk Tea" to kick off "Get Back," then worked in elements from British cabinet member Enoch Powell on the immigration issue of Pakistani. McCartney attacked the anti-immigration movement in song, but felt his lyrics were not strong enough.

Numerous takes of the song were recorded in an effort to get it right; the reprise coda was skipped on one version, but snipped and added from another. Studio manipulation was evident, although that was not the intent of the album. Four official versions of "Get Back" survive: the single, album, *Naked*, and Love recordings. And there is the film version, as well. Each version varies slightly, but most were taken from the sessions of January 27 and 28, 1969.

The inclusion of Billy Preston, whom The Beatles first met in 1962 in Hamburg, added to the harmony of the latter part of the *Get Back* sessions. "Get Back," incidentally, is the only Beatle song that credits another singer, with the exception of Tony Sheridan, listed with The Beatles on "My Bonnie," back in 1962.

"Get Back" reached number one in the US, UK, Canada France Australia, West Germany and Mexico. It was the first Beatles single released in stereo in the States.

During the rooftop performance, The Beatles ran through "Get Back" three times, and in the final version, the police burst onto the roof and switch off the amplifiers. George put them back on so The Beatles could finish their song. That's when Paul says, "Thanks Mo," to Ringo's wife, Maureen Starkey, who was clapping, and John says, "I'd like to thank you…on behalf of the group and myself," and that closes the album and the song and the career of The Beatles in live performances.

"Get Back" was the only Beatle single to enter the charts at Number 1.

(Paul McCartney sang "Get Back" at his Super Bowl half-time performance in 2005; a safe-bet after Janet Jackson went a tad risqué the year before.)

* * *

The genesis of *Let It Be* was in the original concept: to get back to the basics of rock and roll. To that end, The Beatles sought to simplify their recordings, omitting the fanciful studio sounds which predominated in *Pepper*. They wanted to return to their roots.

The challenges to record a live album were almost insurmountable. The effort to capture the creative process of original songs, coupled with the increasing discord within the band, made the task virtually impossible. Three versions of the album were attempted before it was finally released, fifteen months after the final rehearsal.

The first version was to have a cover photo of The Beatles on the EMI stairwell, an update on their 1963 *Please Please Me* album. Glyn Johns prepared a primitive version of the *Get Back* album in March 1969, shortly after the sessions ended. It included the song "Teddy Boy,' by McCartney, plus "Don't Let Me Down." Virtually all the other songs made the final cut, although in varied versions and in a different order. Interestingly, the album opened and closed with "Get Back."

(Several songs which became part of the *Abbey Road* sessions made their initial appearance during *Get Back/Let It Be*. Lennon's "Jealous Guy" and "Gimme Some Truth," Harrison's" All Things Must Pass" and "Hear Me Lord," and McCartney's "Teddy Boy" and "Junk" surfaced in primitive stages during the *Get Back/Let It Be* sessions. If for no other reason, the film is valuable in that it captured the initial composition of these signature songs.)

The Glyn Johns version of the *Get Back* album was modified and re-mixed in April and May of 1969, with a master tape offered to John and Paul. This version contained the song "Save the Last Dance for Me," a rocker instrumental, and similar songs to the other version, including the "Get Back" reprise.

By the time The Beatles heard the basic acetate, they had lost interest in the project and wandered off in different directions. However, a version of the album was played in a few American cities in September 1969, the implication being that the new Beatles album was on its way.

In December 1969, The Beatles asked Glyn Johns to try a second version of the album, but to select solely song versions that had been filmed for the *Get Back* movie, which had not yet been released. George, Paul, and Ringo returned to the recording studio in January 1970 to prepare new mixes for this latest version; John had ostensibly left the group. "Teddy Boy" was omitted, as it had not appeared in the film. (And McCartney himself was double dipping, preparing his own solo album, which included "Teddy Boy.") Without Lennon, the remaining Beatles re-recorded "I Me Mine" and "Across the Universe." Even after these efforts, The Beatles did not approve the final result.

Phil Spector was hired by John, George, and Ringo to resurrect the tapes in a third effort to complete the project. The result was *Let It Be*, with the orchestral wall-of-sound effect. And the rest is history. This effort created as much discord as anything else The Beatles were involved in.

The intent of The Beatles was to get back to their roots, but with the dissolution of the group, *Let It Be* was a more appropriate title for the album than *Get Back*. *Let It Be* engendered the largest advanced sales record at the time of its release, 3.7 million. And yet, for all intents and purposes, The Beatles were no more.

* * *

The January 1969 recording sessions had been both audio and videotaped. George Harrison and John Lennon wanted Phil Spector to produce the album from those tapes, which he did with an additional plush arrangement.

On January 30, 1969, The Beatles performed their much awaited, highly anticipated, but impromptu and hence, unannounced, live concert atop their studio, to the consternation of shopkeepers and Bobbies who had to contend with traffic patterns on the streets below. It proved once more how adept The Beatles were at garnering publicity. And it turned out to be the very last live performance by John, Paul, George, and Ringo. Dramatically captured on film, it was released as the highpoint in the movie version *Let It Be*.

The single "Get Back" was released on April 11, 1969 and fueled excitement that an album would soon be forthcoming. "Get Back" is a hard, loud, fast rock-and-roll song. The title implies a return to their roots, though the story line bears little resemblance to that reality. The song recounts the saga of one enticing Loretta Martin and her travails with California grass. McCartney originally wrote the song as an attack on the influx of Pakistani immigrants descending on British soil, but changed his tune when he realized people would probably think he was serious in his attempt at humor.

The flip side of the single is Lennon's "Don't Let Me Down," a tribute to his lover. "Don't Let Me Down" is sung at a slower pace, yet full of energy and generates a sense of a deeper love than Lennon's odes on *The White Album*. His capacity to bare his soul to the world on behalf of his love is more evident than ever in this wailing melody.

The double-A single rose rapidly up the charts, but no album emerged. A number of songs from the *Get Back* sessions trickled out via bootleg albums, not the way The Beatles intended. A strong case evolved to release the album because bootleg versions of the sessions had been pilfered from Apple studios.

The bootleg tapes were the only indication of Beatle activity in the spring of 1969. Open discord within the group filtered into the press. The need for a new manager to address and supervise the concerns for The Beatles was evident. And that became an issue itself.

Allen Klein made it a point to always get what he wanted. When he learned of the death of Brian Epstein in 1967, Klein set his eye on managing The Beatles. He already had control of Herman's Hermits, the Dave Clark Five, and the Rolling Stones, but he wanted more. He wanted the best.

Klein shared his hand with John Lennon and made a favorable impression. But Paul McCartney had other plans. He wanted his new brother-in-law, Lee Eastman, to manage The Beatles. Neither John nor Paul would compromise. Battle lines were drawn.

Maybe it was a result of Paul's dominance on *The White Album* or his arrogance during the *Get Back* sessions, but John, George and Ringo ganged up to support Allen Klein. Three Beatles out of four voted to authorize Klein to be their manager.

The first problem Klein had to face was to stem the tide of the bootlegs that had seeped out of the *Get Back* sessions. George Harrison wanted assurances all profits rightfully due The Beatles were paid. Klein tried to gain control over NEMS, the shareholding company. He could not do that. Nor could he wrangle copyrights to the songs through the publishing company, Northern Songs.

But Klein was not working for The Beatles as a group; he only had seventy-five percent on his side. Paul McCartney and Lee Eastman wanted to obtain rights to the shareholding and copyright privileges and blocked Klein. At Apple board meetings, the vehemence of each party was evident. There was no cooperation between Klein and Eastman. The Beatles were imploding.

One significant success did result from Allen Klein's efforts. The contract between EMI and The Beatles was rewritten, and granted The Beatles a marked increase on each album sold. Klein's management dispelled talk of Apple bankruptcy, as well.

John Lennon acted on the revitalization of the company when he purchased a country estate for $350,000 in the spring of 1969. He was quoted as saying, "Apple had to pull its socks up—we've done that."

The film canisters of the *Get Back* sessions remained under lock and key. Klein withheld them until he felt the time was right for their release. He brought a semblance of organization to the sprawling miasma of Apple Corps. He limited outsiders and hangers-on who had no business there, and reduced the amount of pounds and wine that flowed out the door.

Of greater interest to the general public than Apple Corps, was the personal agenda of the individual Beatles. Even as Apple pulled up its socks, The Beatles headed off in separate ways, each intent on doing his own thing.

* * *

It was an extremely busy spring for The Beatles. They must have realized that the end of the ride was approaching, and they sought to do it all before it was too late.

The personal lives of John and Paul changed dramatically. Weeks after blithely singing "Two of Us" in the Apple recording studio at Abbey Road, and within two weeks of each other, John and Paul each got married, in their own way, to women who could provide structure to foster their musical talents and a home life each man sought.

By getting married, John and Paul signaled the demise of their song-writing team and created an excuse for the disillusion of the group. Their lives grew further apart as their wives assumed a primary focus.

Paul had met Linda Eastman when he came to New York in the spring of 1968 to announce the formation of Apple Corps. He stayed briefly with her in New York that fall, and they were married on March 12, 1969.

John and Yoko followed suit a week later, with a trip to Gibraltar to formally tie the knot. As Lennon noted, it was, "Perfect. Quick, quiet and British." A month later Lennon changed his middle name, from Winston for the Prime Minister, to Ono, because she had taken his last name.

While Paul and Linda secluded themselves from the press, eventually settling in Scotland to raise sheep and babies, John and Yoko publicized their nuptials to the world with a prominent honeymoon, inviting reporters to their bedroom as they hosted a bed-in for peace in Amsterdam, a bag-in for communication in Vienna, and a triumphant return to London with fifty acorns tied in a bag to distribute to world leaders in a plea for peace.

Hardly anyone knew where Paul and Linda honeymooned, but Beatle fans sang along with "The Ballad of John and Yoko," John's slap-dash recording of his honeymoon. He was so intent on publicity that he wanted to rush the release of his single.

"Get Back" had only just hit the charts when John's new song was recorded, produced and released on May 30, 1969. Ringo was busy filming *The Magic Christian*, and George was tied up elsewhere, so it came down to John and Paul. Listen carefully to catch the potent McCartney drumming and classic over-dubbing which brought the driving beat of the "Ballad" to the forefront of musical pleasure.

Lennon reveled in loud, hard rock and roll and of course invited controversy with his refrain, comparing himself to Jesus Christ. Some AM radio stations blipped these words or refused to play the song. John Lennon didn't care; it garnered more publicity.

John was so excited by the success of his "Ballad" that he repeated his style of reporting in song. "Give Peace a Chance" was recorded during a ten-day Bed-in for Peace in Toronto, and released on the Fourth of July, 1969. Lennon came up with the lyrics spontaneously, and a chorus of roommates, including Dick Gregory, Petula Clark, Tommy Smothers, Murry the K, and Timothy Leary, chimed in on the chorus, which was simply asking the opportunity for peace to prosper.

(In the spring of 2008 a woman who had been in the room during the recording of the song, sold the actual lyrics on e-Bay, so the rest of the world could enjoy them.)

Though written, sung, and recorded by Lennon, the song was credited to Lennon and McCartney, as their thirteen-year agreement required. With the Plastic Ono Band, a pick-up group, John sang his anthem and shared credit. While Lennon was proud of the results of his efforts, the song topped out only at number 14, mediocre by Beatle standards.

"Give Peace a Chance" was sung at peace rallies throughout 1969, and decades later ranks as one of the more popular anti-war anthems. Thousands of marching demonstrators chanted the song in the summer and fall of 1969, as protests expanded against the United States involvement in Vietnam. Lennon attained worldwide recognition when thousands of protesters chanted it on the grounds of the Washington Monument on Moratorium Day in October 1969. He was quite moved by this event.

While John and Yoko were sleeping around for peace, and Paul and Linda were holed up in Scotland, George bit into Zapple. Zapple was the short-lived loony side of Apple Corps, specifically designed to record the likes of Frank Zappa, Allen Ginsberg, and

Ken Kesey. The Beatles intended Zapple to be a catchall for the offbeat, less-popular type of recording. John and Yoko's *Unfinished Music #2, Life with the Lions*, was Zapple's first release in May 1969, followed by George's *Electronic Sound*, an experiment with a Moog synthesizer.

Neither Yoko's 26-minute scream inside a bag, recorded at Cambridge University, nor George's amateur attempts at computerized music, was worthy of The Beatles. Even the covers of the albums were weak: *Unfinished Music* exposed John and Yoko in their hospital room, preceding one of Yoko's miscarriages; George chose childlike finger-painting to decorate his *Electronic Sound*.

Ringo Starr, meanwhile, was busy with Peter Sellers filming *The Magic Christian*. Ringo felt he had a new career as a star of the silver screen, if he could get a few breaks. *The Magic Christian* was his first effort, but over the years he appeared as a minor character in a number of films, none memorable. Incidentally, the music for *The Magic Christian* was written and produced by Paul McCartney for the Apple band, Badfinger.

Paul and George wrote scores for a number of films. Paul penned the songs for *The Family Way* and *Live and Let Die* of James Bond fame. George wrote the score for *Wonderwall* and Monty Python flicks.

John didn't write film scores, but did star in the antiwar movie, *How I Won the War*, in 1967. John and Yoko developed a number of avant-garde films in the 1970s, including *Erection*, a time-lapse photographic vision of the construction of a building, and *Smile*, a video of John smiling. Yoko also filmed a large number of bare derrieres. So much for movies.

So The Beatles headed off in various directions in the summer of 1969. Their private lives changed rapidly. Apple Corps gained a semblance of management under the ruthless rule of Allen Klein, and there was continued conflict between John and Paul over Eastman versus Klein in running the business of The Beatles.

Yet in the middle of the summer of 1969, amid controversy and dissolution, The Beatles gathered once more, one final time, to retreat to the sanctity of Abbey Road and lay down their final tracks. They were together only a few weeks, but the songs they wrote and performed in their final masterpiece proved their best-selling album of all time.

* * *

Carolyn O'Daly (retired registered nurse and freelance writer): *"The years that led up to the summer of love are usually described as tumultuous. I know that's how I felt. The world was changing as rapidly as our bodies and minds. I came of age in the '60s. As you know the '60s is the decade that started in 1964 and ended in 1974. Up until '64 it was still the '50s. After '74 it was the '70s. It was the age of Aquarius, whatever that means, and the decade of sex, drugs, and rock and roll, although I'm sure people had sex before 1964, and there was some very creditable rock and roll before 1964, but drugs? I'm not so sure. I do know that most of my generation tried some pot, at the very least, though some claimed they did not inhale. I also know that my generation included some of the greatest tekkie minds that came down the pike, so we didn't all fry our brains. As usual I'm off the subject.*

"My subject is **Sgt. Pepper's Lonely Heart's Club Band**, *written and performed by The Beatles. Probably the single greatest combination of musical talent in history. They certainly became the wealthiest. But we never begrudged them, since their music gave us so much pleasure. I remember the first time I saw them on the Ed Sullivan Show. I could identify with those screaming fans of Frank Sinatra. The thrill of actually seeing them in person, albeit on a TV screen, after falling deeply in love with their music was so exciting I couldn't sit still. It was music, puppy love, and adoration all rolled into one. Don't call*

me sacrilegious for comparing it to Fatima or Lourdes. We couldn't control our emotions. It was the Pied Piper. It was Beatlemania.

"To this day I don't know what came first, The Beatles or the '60s. I do know that the two are irrevocably entwined in my mind. I can't separate the summer of love from 'All You Need Is Love.' We grew together from gentle kids, 'I Want to Hold Your Hand,' and 'She Loves You Yeah, Yeah, Yeah,' to war protesters and peaceniks' 'Give Peace a Chance' and 'Imagine' (though technically those were just Lennon's). It was the background music of my youth. When I offered to write something for Tom's Beatlefest I had no idea how emotional the trip down memory lane would be.

"Paul McCartney and John Lennon were the poet laureates of the '60s. Their words were the Shakespeare sonnets and Byron odes of our time. **Sgt. Pepper's Lonely Hearts Club Band** was written and performed for all of us who were too chicken to drop acid.

"I was in college in 1967. I can remember going home for dinner, and my father would have the national news on the TV, and Huntley or Brinkley would be announcing the number of dead and maimed in Viet Nam. The paper would have an occasional obit of a former classmate. We were still raw from the assassinations of good people trying to improve our country. We were tired. We were ready for a change. We realized that it wouldn't come without our participation. If four boys from Liverpool could become (more famous than Jesus) then anything was possible. We were the generation that seriously questioned the government. We protested, burned our draft cards and dropped out. (Not all of us, of course, but the message was clear.) 'Make love, not war' became a catch phrase. We burned our bras and demanded equality for all. It was a mini revolution but a revolution nonetheless.

"The Beatles had a song for that, too."

Chapter Eleven: *Abbey Road*—September 26, 1969

Ed Muskie gives our commencement address at Boston University in May of 1969. I have completed my undergraduate experience and enroll at Simmons College for a year in a Master of Arts in Teaching program. Simmons is all female, but allows token males in the graduate school. The program is academically advanced, on the cutting edge of educational challenges, promoting the open classroom and Montessori teaching techniques. I am involved in the peace movement, living with a woman in downtown Boston, engrossed in my world.

During that summer of 1969, a man walks on the moon, and Woodstock nation draws worldwide attention. Ayn Rand paints a picture of two worlds: technology versus hedonism. She contrasts the epitome of intelligence versus the gratuitous sex which she feels leads to the decline of our culture. The age of Apollo is in direct conflict to the decadence of Dionysius.

And The Beatles return, harmoniously, one last time, to the recording studio.

On Friday September 26, 1969, BBC television interrupted scheduled programming to announce that The Beatles had released their latest album, *Abbey Road*.

This was unprecedented recognition of the impact of The

Beatles. Here was free publicity from the established order. It was Britain's nod to their most famous promoter of good will. This was news.

A couple of Beatles were on hand to discuss the album, and a few critics offered constructive comments. When the album was released in the States, it was accompanied by praise from radio stations, news magazines and the daily press. The Beatles had done it again.

Producer George Martin worked closely with Paul McCartney in the arrangement and production of *Abbey Road*. Martin had symphonic tendencies and a majestic composition in mind, and influenced McCartney along those lines. Together they created an orderly, formal musical composition. They were tolerant of Lennon's enthusiasm for basic rock and roll, but McCartney was more conservative.

The contrast is evident in McCartney's "Oh, Darling," which is tight, well-defined, rock versus Lennon's "I Want You/(She's So Heavy)," which meanders, seemingly without end. McCartney imposed control on his own compositions and created a more classic rock album as he reined in Lennon and pushed Harrison and Starr to stellar performances.

Abbey Road was the name of the album, from the name of the street where The Beatles recording studio was located. The album was recorded in just over two weeks, very brief in the creation of a signal album in the late 1960s. *Abbey Road* features The Beatles in three-part harmonies, and straightforward playing, without the orchestral studio backup or electronic experiments that gave *Sgt. Pepper* its unique appeal. The majesty of the album is in the music. It is clear The Beatles were in peak performance during the *Abbey Road* sessions.

They proved themselves masters to the very end. Even on the brink of dissolution—and later interviews indicated they all knew the end was inevitable—they could retreat to the recording studio and pour out their best licks, their most memorable tunes. *Abbey Road* is a symphonic collage of all that made The Beatles the greatest rock group of the 1960s and beyond!

The *Abbey Road* sessions occurred in July of 1969, although the initial impetus for some of the songs surfaced during the *Get Back/Let It Be* sessions in January, and more work was added in April.

From July 2-August 1, 1969, The Beatles rose above their discord and sat down to create their final masterpiece. Their goal was to play the way they had years ago: free-spirited and enthused about their music. By putting aside their differences and devoting themselves to the end goal of what would very likely be their final work, they achieved a success equaled only by…themselves.

Abbey Road debuted at number one in the UK on September 26, and was the best selling album in 1969 in Great Britain. It was considered the fourth-best album of the 1960s. For eleven weeks it held the number-one slot in the United States. *Rolling Stone* magazine considers it the 14th best album of all time.

Abbey Road is the only Beatles album completely recorded on eight track tapes, which produced better sound separation. George Harrison introduced the Moog synthesizer, which figured prominently in several songs.

The name of the album was going to be *Everest*, a popular English cigarette. A photo of the Himalayas would be in the background, but instead The Beatles asked photographer Iain MacMillan to take a few shots of them crossing the street on August 8, 1969. MacMillan only had ten minutes to perform the shoot, and the result is one of the most recognizable covers in the industry, copied and parodied the world over. The zebra crosswalk is a popular tourist destination, though it was modified in the 1970s. The owner of the Volkswagen in the photo often complained of stolen license plates—28 IF—and eventually auctioned the car off for $23,000, to the Volkswagen Museum in Wolfsburg Germany.

The first side of the album is a series of unrelated single songs, each of which stands on its own. The second side opens with a pair of songs, then segues into a medley where one song runs into the next, through to the end. To top it off, The Beatles included an unlisted tune at the end, the shortest song they ever recorded.

"Come Together" was John Lennon's contribution to the California gubernatorial campaign of Timothy Leary: "Come Together, Join the Party." Leary had to drop out of his race against Ronald Reagan when he was arrested and jailed for possession of marijuana, but the song became the first cut on *Abbey Road*. "Come Together" was banned by the BBC for its reference to Coca-Cola, which could be construed as cocaine. Or a commercial advertisement.

Ripe with Lennon's intrigue at writing nonsense verse, "Come Together" was one of the last times all four Beatles gathered together to cut a song together. "Come Together" includes a line literally lifted from Chuck Berry's "You Can't Catch Me," which earned Lennon legal troubles. (To resolve a lingering lawsuit, Lennon recorded a collection of oldies for the song's owner, Morris Levy. Lennon's 1975 *Rock and Roll* album was that payment, for which fans benefitted.)

"Something" was the flip to "Come Together" on the double-A single from *Abbey Road*, the first time George Harrison received that prominence with The Beatles. It is the only Harrison song to top the US charts while he was a Beatle.

"Something" was ostensibly written for Pattie Harrison, George's lover. She also was the inspiration for "Layla," by Eric Clapton, who basically stole Pattie from George. "Something" was written during the *White Album* sessions, in the summer of 1968, but held back.

The first line of "Something" was inspired by Apple's James Taylor who wrote "Something in the Way She Moves." Harrison liked the line and lifted it, a la Lennon; the difference was that Taylor worked for Apple and took it as a compliment. In the recording of "Something," some twenty strings were overdubbed to give the song its richness. The original version lingered nearly eight minutes, with a long instrumental at the end, but was cut down to size.

Lennon considered "Something" the best song on *Abbey Road*, and McCartney thought it was the best song George ever wrote. It certainly ranks with the top love songs by The Beatles, unabashedly frank and sincere in its adoration of a lover. Frank Sinatra said it was his favorite Lennon-McCartney love song; the irony being that it wasn't.

When he wrote it George pictured Ray Charles singing it. Indeed Charles, along with over 150 different musicians, has covered the tune. (The song was in a Chrysler commercial in 1987. At the Concert for George in 2002, Eric Clapton and Paul McCartney sang it with accompaniment. Bob Dylan sang the song in a memorial to George, who was a member of the Traveling Wilburys.)

The third song on the album, McCartney's "Maxwell's Silver Hammer," premiered during the *Get Back/Let It Be* sessions. A couple of unique sounds can be heard as George Harrison played the Moog and Ringo Starr banged an anvil.

"Maxwell's Silver Hammer" was written in a vaudeville style, light, lively and bouncy. The song recounts the exploits of Maxwell Edison who used his hammer to knock down and kill his girlfriend Joan, his teacher, then the judge. McCartney wrote this ironic diatribe to show how bad things could get, a dark drama of black humor.

Lennon was in hospital in Scotland, recovering from an auto accident on July 1-6, 1969, when this song was recorded, so he (mercifully, for his sake) missed the session. He despised the song;

Harrison thought it had a catchy tune. Starr denigrated that session as the worst of The Beatles' career.

McCartney found his "Oh! Darling" difficult to sing, so he performed it only once a day, to preserve his voice. Lennon thought he personally should have sung lead; it was more his style. The lyrics are not as strong as the music; McCartney's intentionally hoarse and strained voice carries the song.

Ringo wrote "Octopus's Garden" when he broke from the group in August 1968 to go off on holiday in Sardinia. While onboard ship, he was offered an octopus sandwich but turned it down. The captain regaled him with tales that an octopus will scrounge along the ocean floor, seeking shiny objects to line its nest. Ringo had the genesis for his song. It was considered one of his best tunes, light and charming, and enjoyed by all.

George helped Ringo on the harmony as witnessed during the *Get Back/Let It Be* sessions. Unusual sound effects were accomplished when the back-up voices of George and Paul were compressed to produce a gurgling sound. Ringo blew through a straw in a glass of water to create the sound of bubbles.

John Lennon spliced two songs together in "I Want You (She's So Heavy)," following the *Get Back/Let It Be* sessions. With only fourteen words, and repeated guitar chords, the song extended nearly eight minutes, making this the second longest song, next only to "Revolution 9" in The Beatles repertoire.

Lennon was strongly influenced by progressive rock in this song, with white noise and repeated guitar riffs. Harrison played the Moog synthesizer, and the guitars were overdubbed. The song is imitative of a blues riff that continues ad infinitum. Lennon wanted the song to end abruptly, and signaled engineer Geoff Emerick to cut it at the 7:44 minute mark, leaving the end of the song, and the first side of the album with a jarring break.

Ironically, "I Want You (She's So Heavy)" was one of the last songs The Beatles recorded together, so its abrupt ending, recorded on August 20, 1969, signaled the end of The Beatles as a musical entity.

On side two, "Here Comes the Sun" was arguably one of George Harrison's best-known compositions, written while relaxing in Eric Clapton's garden after a tedious Apple Corporation meeting. Harrison was fed up with the acrimony of accounting aspects in the music empire and needed a respite. He found it in Clapton's garden, and unburdened his emotions. Winter was almost over; spring was near. The song has a hopeful, happy feeling.

(Harrison performed "Here Comes the Sun" on *Saturday Night Live* with Paul Simon on November 20, 1976. Lennon and McCartney were in New York at the time, together, watching the show. Lorne Michaels, the *SNL* maven, tried to get The Beatles back together, dangling a $3000 offer, union wages, to get the group on stage again. But, as we know, it was just a dream.)

John Lennon penned his sonorous ballad "Because" on hearing Yoko pick out the notes of Beethoven's "Moonlight Sonata" on the piano. He asked her to play the chords backwards, and the song was born, or so the story goes.

"Because" bears the influence of a Moog synthesizer, as well as the unique three-part harmony of John, Paul, and George, triple-tracked, to produce the sound of nine voices. It is the only Beatle song with three singers throughout; no solos. This gave the song a Beach Boys feel. The three Beatles sat together on a bench, during the session, and Ringo moved in to sit with them. One can picture this scene as one of their final happy moments together, smiling as they sang along.

"Because" segues into a medley—a sixteen-minute session of unfinished song snippets—strung together in a suite which concludes *Abbey Road*. Many refrains from these tunes can be heard in the *Get Back/Let It Be* sessions.

"You Never Give Me Your Money" is McCartney's take on the financial antagonism that continued to roil The Beatles as they wrangled over the management of Apple Corps. Funny paper refers to the amount of money The Beatles were worth "on paper" rather than money in the bank.

A couple of riffs in "You Never Give Me Your Money" repeat on "Carry That Weight," and pieces of Harrison's "Here Comes the Sun" resurface. To add to the repetition, Lennon's "Sun King" was originally titled "Here Comes the Sun King," but the title was shortened to avoid confusion, though the first line is the same as Harrison's song. The song supposedly came to Lennon in a dream. The original name was "Los Paranoias."

George Martin played with channel surfing in "Sun King," switching from left to right speaker in stereo. Lennon introduced a few Spanish and Italian words to sound cosmopolitan. The Beatles toyed with the Fleetwood Mac reverb sound of "Albatross," but didn't pursue it. "Sun King" has a charming over-dubbed three-part harmony that leads into a strong drumbeat.

"Mean Mr. Mustard" was written during The Beatles trip to India, early in 1968, and was considered for inclusion on *The White Album*. Lennon thought of it as a throwaway tune, based on a newspaper story about an anti-social miserly man. The sister was originally named Shirley, but became Pam when The Beatles were assembling the suite and "Polythene Pam" was the next song in the sequence, so it eased the transition.

Like "Mustard," "Polythene Pam" was considered during the *White Album* sessions, but withheld at the time. Lennon's "Polythene Pam" referenced a night of kinky sex when Lennon, poet Royston Ellis, and his girlfriend Stephanie, attired in plastic bags, got into bed together. We'll leave the rest to your imagination. The "News of the World" is a tabloid, which recounted risqué activities by the fast set. The limerick is sung in a strong

Liverpudlian accent, different from the more Americanized accent of The Beatles.

"Polythene Pam" segues, without pause, directly into "She Came in Through the Bathroom Window." "She Came in Through the Bathroom Window" actually happened to a member of the Moody Blues, who told the tale to Paul McCartney, who wrote the song. Or maybe it happened to Paul himself; the origins are a little sketchy. A Diane Ashley claims to have been the girl who crept into the McCartney household in 1968. She is now married with four children, and has a photo hanging in her kitchen of herself with Paul, bearing testament to her days as an Apple Scruff.

"Golden Slumbers" was written by McCartney, based on a 17th century poem by Thomas Dekker. Paul composed this lullaby in his youth, sitting at his stepsister's piano, unable to read music. "Golden Slumbers" was recorded at the same time as the subsequent song, without a break.

"Carry That Weight" employed all four Beatle singing the chorus in a vocal harmony, a rarity in their recordings. The song reprised the melody of "You Never Give Me Your Money" with guitar riffs reminiscent of Harrison's "Here Comes the Sun."

The meat of "Carry That Weight" lies in its lyrics. McCartney wrote the song about the situation The Beatles found themselves in at the end of that ponderous decade. On one level, McCartney implied that if Lennon left the group, as he threatened to, he would carry the weight of the break-up for the rest of his life. Another take is that McCartney had assumed leadership of The Beatles after Brian Epstein died, and the financial and musical direction was too much for him. No longer could he carry the weight for the success of The Beatles. And a third interpretation is that the song refers to The Beatles as individuals, knowing they were going to break up, and would never accomplish as much alone as they had as a group.

The song is laced with inner meanings and varied interpretations, typical of so much of their work.

"Ending" was the working title for "The End," which was intended to close out the album. McCartney wanted each of The Beatles to perform their distinctive style. Ringo did his drum solo, the only one he ever recorded in a Beatle song. Next comes a series of repeating guitar solos, first by Paul, then George, and John, which capture the essence of their individual styles. McCartney had each perform their specialty, his being the straight string bends, Harrison's the more technically advanced picking, and Lennon's the distorted, stinging sounds. The song concludes with a thirty-piece orchestra and includes the lyric sung nearly two dozen times.

The final couplet describes the love you take matching the love you make. This line brings a tight conclusion to the song, to the album, and to The Beatles' career. Nothing is left hanging.

Except for "Her Majesty." "Her Majesty" was a filler intended to fit between "Mean Mr. Mustard" and "Polythene Pam." McCartney didn't like it, and discarded it, literally tossing the snippet of tape on the floor. Engineer John Kurlander, taught never to throw anything away, picked it up and spliced it at the end of the medley. McCartney liked it, and it became part of history.

"Her Majesty" opens with the ending chord of "Mean Mr. Mustard" and closes abruptly, because the final note had already been recorded in "Polythene Pam." Thus, the songs on both sides of the album end abruptly, leaving the listener hungering for more.

Still in its rough mix, "Her Majesty" begins on the hard-right stereo speaker and moves across to hard left, making a brief rendition of studio technology, easy to appreciate.

"Her Majesty" is the shortest song in The Beatles repertoire, lasting a mere 23 seconds. The last-minute inclusion of the song on the album caught record producers off guard, as the song title was omitted from the initial printing of the album sleeve.

(Paul McCartney sang "Her Majesty" for Queen Elizabeth at Buckingham Palace Gardens in 2002 in honor of her golden jubilee.)

And that was it. John Lennon left the group in September 1969, and in January 1970 Paul, George, and Ringo doctored up some of the *Get Back* songs and handed the masters over to Phil Spector. Spector upset McCartney with his arrangement of "Let It Be" in the spring of 1970 when he added a choir of fourteen women, a string orchestra, and a horn section. McCartney was outraged, and demanded the accompaniments be removed. Spector refused, and a week later McCartney broke from The Beatles, using the mistreatment of this song as one of his excuses to leave the group.

McCartney's break, the fourth and final Beatle to leave the band, was irrevocable, since he did it in public, with a solo album and accompanying interview.

Ironically, the issue of the distortion of "Let It Be" erupted because Spector was displeased with John Lennon's bass playing. Lennon never played bass in a Beatle recording, and apparently was pretty bad. Spector tried to bury his miscues. The song took a wayward turn, though it still captured the number-one slot. ("Let It Be" was stripped of adornments and re-released in McCartney's original format in 2003 on *Let It Be...Naked*.)

And that's where the pieces fell in the spring of 1970 as McCartney left The Beatles. The *Let It Be* sessions were sublimated by the dissolution of the group, and the album was released half-heartedly the next month. And that was it.

* * *

Reverend Jerry Fritz officiated at a wedding on Martha's Vineyard. Must have been 500 people. One of them was Paul McCartney: *"One of the things I was surprised at was his graciousness. He* *was talking with the bride's grandfather. We talked ten or fifteen minutes and had a glass of champagne. I expected he would not be so concerned or interested in me. It was easy to speak with him."*

Reverend Fritz continued. *"McCartney's brother-in-law, John Eastman, was related to the groom. I was in awe. I grew up with The Beatles, sure, I always enjoyed their music. This was one of those once-in-a lifetime things. It's a very Vineyard story. He stuck around. I had three weddings that day. He stayed all evening, and I heard [that later that evening] he broke out a guitar and sang to the group."*

Then there's the unnamed woman who made eye-contact with Paul McCartney when he attended this Vineyard wedding. That's a memory she'll always treasure.

Epilogue: It Was 40 Years Ago Today

On the day I get married, April 18, 1970, I pick up an album entitled **McCartney** *and realize, as I scan the interview inside, that as I commit to my new wife, The Beatles have broken up, never to play together again. It is a poignant moment in my life.*

As they evolved in their struggle for self-realization, The Beatles came to symbolize the aspirations of the under-thirty generation in the 1960s. To ideally comprehend this phenomena, one must have "grown up" with them; that is to say, been aware of what their songs meant when you first heard them, integrating their message into your own stage in life: in short, coming of age with The Beatles.

The Beatles matured with their audience and, time and again, verbalized issues key to so many baby boomers of the 1960s. With their popularity, The Beatles assumed a powerful role as spokesmen for a generation. They found their niche in the increasingly alienated youth of the 1960s.

What they wrote for public consumption is open for discussion. Marijuana busts, comparisons with Jesus, marriages and movies are tabloid fodder. What The Beatles said in their songs, their communication to a generation, is their lasting legacy. That their songs still receive airplay, decades after their last album, is testimony to the enduring appreciation of their music.

The Beatles were a phenomenon not only in music, but in the social fabric of our society. One becomes acquainted with them, not merely through biography, but in understanding the culture that encouraged them, the generation that adopted them and the established order that balanced them between praise in their prowess while criticizing their avant-garde message.

* * *

In the decade after The Beatles dissolved in the spring of 1970, the press and the public coyly hoped and fervently prayed The Beatles would reunite, if just for one grand concert. The sudden, sad shooting of John Lennon on the doorstep of his New York home on December 8, 1980, brought an abrupt end to those hopes and dreams. And the generation that latched onto The Beatles in the wake of the assassination of President Kennedy was once more faced with the horror and sorrow of assassination. Even as The Beatles brought hope to the ideals of a disaffected youth, the death of John Lennon sealed their fate as idols and ideals of our collective youth.

* * *

I never made it to a Beatles concert, but …

I did see George Harrison fill the old Boston Garden for a concert, back in 1970. He sat on the floor of the stage and played with Ravi Shankar. It was an impressive performance, though so different from The Beatles. I was taken aback, but it was great to see him.

I took my daughters, Amy and Jill, to the old Foxboro Stadium, for a Paul McCartney and Wings concert. He was great, but what I remember were the vendors selling tee-shirts they had smuggled under their coats. I saw McCartney in concert in Worcester, with a stage section that rose when he sang "Fool on the Hill." McCartney was great, but he wasn't The Beatles.

I saw Ringo at Harbor Lights in Boston, and also at Great Woods, attired in a great coat, looking like a ringmaster in a circus. His voice was unmistakable. And with a new song, "Liverpool 8," and his perennial All-Starr Band, he is still on the concert circuit.

One of my great regrets is never o have heard John Lennon sing or play. I've been to Strawberry Fields in Central Park several times, but never heard or saw the great man. (But then, my wife Joyce is a big Elvis fan, and she never saw the King either.)

* * *

I loaned a precursor of this manuscript, my only copy, to classmate Howie Broomfield, back in the late '60s. He promised to read it and get back to me with comments. He married and moved to Canada, and it was years before I retrieved my tattered pages. I reworked the story, printed it, and distributed it to friend and family in Gloucester, in 1982. And now, twenty-five-plus years later, I have again rewritten this Beatle project.

* * *

In 1980 in my training as a nursing-home administrator, I made a video of institutionalized young people, traumatized by incapacitating injuries. They were severely challenged, both mentally and physically. I shot a video of their daily lives for promotional purposes. As a soundtrack, I used "In My Life." It was a powerful piece.

The night John Lennon died, I was at my brother George's, to select a Christmas tree. I left the house near midnight, turned on the radio, and heard the tragic words about the shooting of John Lennon. I returned to my brother's house. Stanley was still there, and we comforted each other. My brother went to bed. Stanley left. I remember lying on a cot, emotionally drained, as that night went on forever. I had not cried when Kennedy died, but there were tears on my pillow when I awoke the next day. That evening, December 9, 1980, I spent a half hour with Bob Murphy and Art Devine, watching Walter Cronkite devote the entire CBS evening news to the tragic death of John Lennon. It was an endless day.

In 1998 I chaperoned a school group of West Tisbury eighth graders through the Beatle Museum in Liverpool. We wandered through the rooms of this wondrous building, with a mock-up of the Cavern nightclub, and photos of The Beatles, from way back when to their days of fame and glory. The kids were impressed. Beatle music played in the background. I treasure the memories of that trip to Liverpool with Joyce.

In 2007 I assembled a 40th anniversary tribute for **Sgt. Pepper** at the Katharine Cornell Theatre in Vineyard Haven on Martha's Vineyard. It was great to recall how impressive The Beatles were, and the impact they made on our generation. Their music was key to my growing up, and some of these memories linger because of the music I heard at the time.

* * *

The Beatles captured the essence of an emotional experience. Superb word smiths, creative musicians, they rode the route to fame and fortune, the vanguard to the '60s, developing a repertoire of memorable melodies that resonate to this day.

Music of The Beatles lives on, in iPods, on the radio, and on old 33-rpm records. It is alive and well in selected universities. Glenn Gass is a professor of music at Indiana University in Bloomington. He writes, "*Yes, the Beatles are as popular as ever! In fact, my classes (360 students) fill up more quickly now then 10 years ago, probably because we have reached critical mass with the baby boomers' children. I've been teaching the course since 1982 and it is a constant joy.*"

John Stevens teaches "The Music of John Lennon" at Berklee College of Music in Boston. This songwriting course is as popular as when he first started to teach it in 1981. Stevens is also the author (with Susan Gedutis Lindsay) of *The Songs of John Lennon: The Beatle Years*. (Berklee Press, 297 pages, 2002)

* * *

Kevin Begley (Vineyard carpenter): *"The greatest kick to me is that you can still put any one of their discs on today and feel the energy, poetry, and passion come crackling through to make the hair on the back of your neck stand up, your feet dance, your voice sing, your eyes cry, your heart fill up and overflow. They gave us so much. Thanks forever, gentlemen."*

Op Ed piece from Vineyard Gazette—May 25, 2007
It Was Forty Years Ago Today
by Tom Dresser

I picked up the West Tisbury baseball team last week, adding them to the complement of students already on my bus. As the players bounded aboard, there was a palpable sense of awe. The younger children sat silently and stared at the crisp, bright uniforms. The older students displayed quiet reserve toward their peers, though they ride with them every day. What set them apart? Something about men in uniform.

Flashback forty years ago. I was traveling through Europe, after my sophomore year in college. First stop, London. I took in the fancy shops on Carnaby Street and Piccadilly Circus. I came to a record shop, stopped, and stared in the window. There was a record album, *Sgt. Pepper's Lonely Hearts Club Band*, open for all to see, and gazing out at me were

John, Paul, George, and Ringo in bright, flashy uniforms. I was awestruck.

For the next three months I hitchhiked and Eurailed through Europe. *Sgt. Pepper* was released at the onset of that summer of love. I heard snippets of songs, read clips in the press, and in an Amsterdam record store listened to "All You Need is Love." Those were the days well before iPods, CDs, or cassettes. It was not until I returned stateside in September that I listened to the album in its entirety.

Like most babyboomers, I played it more than once. Shelley Christiansen was a student at Syracuse University and recalls, "You didn't have to buy the album. They played it in the dorms. Over and over. You got to know the words by heart."

What set *Pepper* apart? Was it the dynamic cover with the collage of people who influenced The Beatles from Bob Dylan to Edgar Allen Poe to Marlon Brando? Was it the epaulets which fell out of the jacket when you opened it? Or the words to the songs on the back, a novelty at the time.

The music was arranged in concert format. We hear the audience settle down at the beginning of the record, then clap at the end. One song flows seamlessly into the next. The tunes touch topics that resonate today: the virtues of friendship, the dismay of a runaway, a fling with a girl, an ode to old age, the search for meaning in life, and the depth of despair in death. And of course *Pepper* catered to the drug culture, and provided an outlet for John Lennon's nonsense verse.

Teaching in Pennsylvania years ago, Betsy Dripps recalls she had a student named, you guessed it, Sergeant Pepper.

When *Pepper* was released on June 1, 1967, the oldest Beatle, Ringo Starr, was not yet 27.

Sgt. Pepper covered tremendous musical territory. The Beatles spent nearly 700 hours to produce 37 minutes of the finest music of the era. It was a signal event for the generation who came of age in the late 1960s. It influenced rock music for generations. And it was a midpoint apex in The Beatles' stellar career. They burst onto the American scene on the Ed Sullivan Show in February 1964, released *Pepper* in 1967, and parted company in April 1970. Their tenure was brief, but their impact impressive.

West Tisbury's Cynthia Riggs recalls she first heard Beatle songs while she was onboard ship, and a research assistant played the tunes again and again.

So where were you forty years ago? What impact did *Sgt. Pepper* make on you? Do you sing along when the songs come on the radio? Is the album on your iPod?

Celebrate forty years since the release of *Sgt. Pepper* with an evening of fun at the Katharine Cornell Theater on Wednesday May 30th, 2007 at 7 p.m. Bring recollections of when you first heard a special Beatle song. Which is your favorite tune? This program is designed to be a fun raiser, not a fundraiser. In the immortal words on the *Pepper* album, "a splendid time is guaranteed for all."

* * *

My View from the *Gloucester Daily Times*—December 8, 1982.
Two Years Ago Today
By Tom Dresser

It was two years ago today that a disturbed man with a gun tragically cut the life of John Lennon short. The wit and wisdom of the foremost rock-music group of the 1960s, an innovative, influential social critic died two months after his 40th birthday.

As a baby-boomer, my adolescence was influenced by the charisma and excitement of The Beatles. I remember watching the Ed Sullivan Show on a borrowed black-and-white TV in February 1964, and raving about The Beatles in school the next day. Driving around in a '47 Plymouth I harmonized with John and Paul on "I Want to Hold Your Hand."

The movie *Hard Day's Night* transferred The Beatles from vinyl to video, and the hectic hysteria of their lives captivated me. Beatle songs proved intellectually and socially stimulating with the likes of "Nowhere Man," "Only Sleeping" and "Help!," proof positive that Lennon/McCartney had more to offer than the hyped hopes of their original "Can't Buy Me Love" songs. The 1965 Baroque music of *Rubber Soul* with melodic, string-backed love ballads, still receives substantive radio play today.

I celebrated Christmas, 1965, exchanging copies of *Rubber Soul* with my two brothers. Even our parents were impressed with the social conscience of "Eleanor Rigby." My memories of dormitory life include the subtle rhythms and allusions of "Strawberry Fields Forever."

Traveling abroad alone in the summer of 1967—he's leaving home—hiking down Penny Lane and along Abbey Road, I hitched a ride with a truck driver who claimed to have known Ringo Starr, and listened to "All You Need Is Love" in an Amsterdam record store. Returning home, bearded and affecting Lennon's rimless eyeglasses (I have 20-20 vision), I was both inspired and invigorated by my personal *Magical Mystery Tour*. The splendor and magnificence of *Sgt. Pepper* epitomized my feelings of loneliness and optimism, and captured relevant transcendental concepts.

Nineteen hundred sixty-eight found me following George Harrison down "Blue Jay Way" and through Haight-Ashbury. I delved enthusiastically into the lyrics and intimations of *The White Album*. As I was maturing, fighting conformity with independence, The Beatles seemed to speak directly to me. My life seemed to parallel The Beatles: at major stages The Beatles would clarify and dignify my emotions in song.

"Give Peace a Chance" became the theme song of the anti-war movement in 1969. John Lennon was said to be moved to tears as he witnessed 100,000 protesters chanting his song on the grounds of the Washington Monument. I marched down Commonwealth Avenue, Peace placard in hand.

Suddenly it was 1970, and the dream was dying. Paul McCartney, the practical lyricist of the most inspired Beatle love songs: "All My Loving," "Yesterday" and "Hey Jude," determined it was time to make a break on his own. And the whole was proven greater than the individual parts.

When McCartney broke the news that "the dream was over," I was already heading off in other directions: marriage, career, home, and children. I was grown up, just as The Beatles had outgrown themselves.

Beatle songs have continued to influence me over the past dozen years. I used the lyrics of their songs to teach children to read. I wrote an essay interpreting the social relevance of their songs. Among friends and colleagues I am known as a Beatle aficionado.

But it is the precious memories of Beatle songs that impacted and influenced me at different stages of my adolescence that I treasure most. And that is why the anniversary of the death of John Lennon strikes a heart-rending chord in me. While we cannot regain the past, we may appreciate the memorable musical moments associated with days gone by.

In Memoriam

Brian Epstein died August 27, 1967
Mal Evans died January 5, 1976
John Lennon died December 8, 1980
George Harrison died November 29, 2001
Neil Aspinall died March 22, 2008

Also by Thomas Dresser:

Dogtown: A Village Lost in Time—1995
Beyond Bar Harbor—1996
It Happened in Haverhill—1996
Looking at Lawrence—1997
Tommy's Tour of the Vineyard—2005
Mystery on the Vineyard—2008
In My Life—2009

For further information, contact Tom at thomasdresser.com

Author's Biography

Tom Dresser came of age in the '60s. Massachusetts borne and bred, Tom lives in Oak Bluffs on Martha's Vineyard with his wife Joyce. He has two daughters, Amy Dresser Held of Los Angeles, and Jill Dresser, of New Orleans, three step-children, Jeremy, Jennifer, and Christopher, and two granddaughters, Shealyn Smyth and Molly Rose Held.

Tom drives a school bus, a tour bus, and a limo, and works at a local art gallery. He writes for the Island Press. Tom and Joyce enjoy hiking and kayaking.

For further information, contact Tom at thomasdresser.com